Quarterly Essay

Quarterly Essay is published four times a year by Black Inc., an imprint of Schwartz Books Pty Ltd. Publisher: Morry Schwartz.

ISBN 9781760644147 ISSN 1444-884x

Subscriptions – 1 year print & digital (4 issues): $79.99 auto-renewing within Australia incl. GST. Outside Australia $134.99. 2 years print & digital (8 issues): $159.99 within Australia incl. GST. 1 year digital only: $49.99.

Payment may be made by Mastercard or Visa, or by cheque made out to Schwartz Books. Payment includes postage and handling.

To subscribe, fill out and post the subscription card or form inside this issue, or subscribe online:

quarterlyessay.com
subscribe@blackincbooks.com
Phone: 61 3 9486 0288

Correspondence should be addressed to:

The Editor, Quarterly Essay
22–24 Northumberland Street
Collingwood VIC 3066 Australia
Phone: 61 3 9486 0288 / Fax: 61 3 9011 6106
Email: quarterlyessay@blackincbooks.com

Editor: Chris Feik. Management: Elisabeth Young. Publicity: Anna Lensky. Design: Guy Mirabella. Associate Editor: Kirstie Innes-Will. Assistant Editor: Rebecca Bauert. Production Coordinator: Marilyn de Castro. Typesetting: Typography Studio.

Printed in Australia by McPherson's Printing Group. The paper used to produce this book comes from wood grown in sustainable forests.

LONE
WOLF

Albanese and the
new politics

Katharine Murphy

On election night in Marrickville, Anthony Albanese cooked dinner at home for some of his staff. His friend, Labor's Senate leader, Penny Wong, asked to come over. In 2019, she had been marooned on an election-night panel on the ABC and had to endure the horrors of losing an election she'd hoped to win in front of hundreds of thousands of viewers. It was excruciating. She vowed never to put herself in that position again. Wong wanted to be with Albanese, come what may. "If we win, you might want me to do something, and if we don't, you might want a friend," she told him. Albanese prepared pasta. On the biggest professional night of his life, he received her in his Newtown Jets football jumper and ugg boots.

Election day had been brutal. Scott Morrison made one last desperate lunge for power by warning voters asylum seekers from Sri Lanka had been intercepted on the high seas. The Liberal Party followed up with text messages to voters in marginal seats. A year earlier, Morrison had sworn himself in as home affairs minister without telling the incumbent, Karen Andrews. Morrison's agents berated public servants to get the word out about the new boat. Faced with unreasonable demands from overwrought pugilists, public servants fell back on process. There was the caretaker convention.

In Operation Sovereign Borders, Morrison's securitised construct, there were lawful chains of command. They asked for an explicit instruction from their minister. The officials had no idea about Morrison's administrative side hustle, shadowing Andrews in the portfolio. Neither, for that matter, did Andrews. The final hours of desperate men were what they always are. Unworthy of the memoir.

After the polls closed on the east coast, the early results didn't look great for Labor. But as the night wore on, it was clear one manifestation of old politics – an armada of illegals on unauthorised boats, Manchurian candidates in the parliament, anti-corruption commissions as a "fringe issue," the "technology not taxes" non sequitur, sports rorts, car park rorts, "I don't hold a hose, mate" – was past tense. Progressivism had spent a decade waiting out the Coalition's war on process and on sense, crouching behind couches, subsisting in bomb shelters with basic rations. When the polls opened on 21 May 2022, centre-right and centre-left progressives sharpened their pencils and crept out of their fortifications with lethal intent. By evening, a red, teal and green mist was rolling through Sydney, across the electorates of Wentworth, North Sydney, Bennelong, Reid and Mackellar; through Melbourne, across Goldstein, Higgins and Kooyong; through inner-city Brisbane, in Adelaide, and in Perth.

The result was more than the unremarkable transfer of power from blue to red. It was an electoral earthquake. The Albanese government would come to power with a primary vote in the low thirties. The Liberal Party had been smashed in the inner city because of an exodus of women and educated professionals. The crossbench in the House of Representatives had swelled to sixteen. More Greens. More independents.

The political insurgents of 2022 heralded more than the end of a tired government. They promised Australians a new kind of politics. Clean and green. Idealistic. Transformational. People-powered. Metropolitan and some regional voters had rallied around an idea that representative democracy could be different. Albanese would be permitted to govern in his own right, but in an altered political landscape.

Albanese is an outsider who became an avid institutionalist, a Labor parliamentarian fluent in more than a century of tradition in Australia's oldest political party. Master of factions and fractions. The architect of countless abstruse organisational intrigues. The great survivor of the regicidal arena. The Labor man had blasted his way to the top at a point of deep fatigue and malaise with major-party politics. Election day 21 May brought victory, but not winner-takes-all, because the new politics zeitgeist wouldn't allow that, not if the survivor intended to go on surviving.

Albanese means to survive. The tide might be going out on the major-party era, but Albanese wants to entrench Labor as the natural party of government at the federal level. That's his ambition. That's his unfinished business. He wants to lay the foundation for a long-term Labor government, not necessarily with him at the apex. Albanese is a politician at his peak. But at nearly sixty, he's entered the final season of his political life. This quest for power isn't rote. It has purpose. Albanese believes Labor is the party of change. I say belief, not faith, because Albanese believes in what he can see. Labor governments made his life better.

In Albanese's youth, change meant moving hard and fast, crushing forces that would thwart him. Experience has taught him subjugation might be victory, but it is not change. Change happens when free minds change. Change requires time, patience and persuasion. Watching Tony Abbott obliterate elements of the Rudd/Gillard reform project taught Albanese nothing persists until a majority of people see that its time has come. Important things can be erased from the record with a stroke of a pen.

Albanese's plan to claw back legitimacy and lay the ground for an extended period of Labor government pushes against the mega-trend of major-party depletion. It might be impossible. He might lack the required fleetness of foot. He's confident, so he might succumb to hubris, the Achilles heel of prime ministers. He might forget important things he learnt about leadership during Opposition. Change requires public investment, and the Labor government has little money to spend. Political journalism can be febrile, shallow and obsessed with spectacle. Albanese lacks the obvious X-factor; he's not a showman. It's likely his project will be mis-understood. Events, domestic or international or both, might cruel his prime ministership. Confidants might betray him. His colleagues might cut him down for just cause, or for sport.

While the world got more dangerous, while domestic needs became more acute, Australia spent a decade marking time because the Coalition was fractured, and directionless, and when it came to facing the existential challenge of the age – the climate crisis – feckless. Voters might now be too impatient to let a new Labor prime minister creep up on them slowly and engage them more quietly. They might scorn Albanese's attempt to defy gravity; his retro desire to make the old politics new.

He might fail. But he will try.

FEAR AND LOATHING IN EAST GOSFORD AND MARRICKVILLE

This is a story about chaos and stillness. As I boarded Albanese's press bus early on 3 May 2022, pundits were in overdrive about whether today would be the day Morrison lost the federal election. These prognostications were pegged to the precedent of 2007. The talking heads noted the Reserve Bank of Australia hiked the cash rate during the 2007 election, and John Howard lost. Interest rates up, incumbents down. Ipso facto. Quod erat demonstrandum.

Weaving past the cameras, bags and bent backsides in the aisle of the bus, I wasn't yet minutely locked on what the RBA governor, Philip Lowe, might or might not do at 2 p.m. Washed in the general ambience, I was also floating, untethered, in the moment. Big day. Bad day. Portents. Do a live cross from the campaign bus. Try not to sway.

I was travelling with Mike Bowers, *Guardian Australia*'s photographer-at-large. We were there to conduct a mid-campaign interview with Albanese. As we rolled out of the city towards the electorate of Robertson, on the NSW Central Coast, with Labor press wrangler Alex Beech doing the daily roll call up the front, Bowers and I were in a huddle about logistics. We needed to get to a house in Gosford, get all the gear off the bus, half do the press conference, but also get around to the front of the house before the conference ended so we could vanish into the motorcade without causing a ruckus. I would knock off the interview in the back of the car between East Gosford and Marrickville. Mike would shoot some new portraits on the way and then back at the Albanese home.

Bowers insisted we shoot a portrait of Albanese and his dog, Toto. Albanese's press office hedged, because that would mean a stopover in Marrickville. There was no particular hostility to the idea; the problem was a portrait in Albo country would take time they didn't have. It was also an incursion on the candidate's private space, and Albanese's unobserved universe was shrinking as he closed in on the prime ministership.

Bowers held out for the image because Albanese adores the dog (or *that bloody dog*, as some of his colleagues prefer) like a child. The cavoodle has been Albanese's constant companion through the roller-coaster of recent existence. If this was to be his last portrait as Opposition leader – and one way or another, win or lose, we both knew it would be – Bowers was determined to capture Odysseus with his talisman.

The Gosford visit was structured around Labor's new "help to buy" scheme – a housing initiative that had been the centrepiece of the campaign launch in Perth a couple of days earlier. Journalists spilled off the bus onto the front lawn of the suburban house and trudged around the back to set up for a press conference under the Hills hoist.

Daily combat between the press pack and the candidate had descended into pub trivia. The atmosphere was oppressive. It seemed possible someone could ask Albanese to recite all the elements of the periodic table, and if he fluffed the answer it would be the lead story on the television news. In Gosford, the provocation was minor. A Sky News reporter asked whether he'd sell one of his investment properties to increase Australia's housing stock. I can't remember the answer. I suspect it was, "Next question."

We joined the motorcade without incident. After a time weaving through the backblocks of Gosford, we stopped at a local coffee shop. The wranglers deemed that an opportunity to get some pictures in the can, sending Bowers into a scramble. Albanese loitered by the water's edge, pale in the sun in his sharp dark suit. A pelican surveyed the Labor leader.

Locals zero in. Incoming – a sixty-something prosperous-looking man. My guess is Morrison supporter. Looks like a self-funded retiree. I can see Albanese bracing, one eye on me, the other on the man, then a furtive glance at Bowers gambolling across the carpark with his camera and a light under his arm.

This isn't an official event. The venue and surrounds have not been advanced. No hecklers have been ejected from the scene. Reality is coming in hot. *The country needs a change. Get this done*, the bloke says to the Labor leader, to the astonishment of all of us. Albanese relaxes instantly. He advises his new friend to persuade a couple of his friends, particularly given we are in Robertson, a Liberal-held marginal seat. The local looks confused. Albanese translates: if you think Scott Morrison needs to go, engage your friends and send a few more votes my way. Elections are a numbers game. This is clearly a new thought. He's clearly a civilian.

We make our way to the café. Bowers takes some shots of Albanese and partner Jodie Haydon having coffee while locals mill around. A bloke in high-vis walks past with a scowl, shaking his head. It's not clear whether the problem is the coffee or the candidate. A woman engages me, and gestures at Albanese. "He's going to win, right?" I shrug, noncommittal. She looks stricken. "Surely he'll win," she insists. "Morrison can't win, surely." I shrug again. "It's tough for Labor to win." That's all I've got. She looks crushed.

With the caffeine inhaled, we scramble out of the café and head back to Sydney. There is communication between the cars. We pull over at a rest stop. Haydon is ejected from Albanese's car and I am in. The interview ensues with scenery whipping past. I'm posing questions and listening closely to answers, but in some part of my head I'm a kid again in the back seat of Mum's car during one of the many trips we did between northern New South Wales and Sydney. There's also a message from the news editor: can I write some commentary for this evening, assuming the bank hikes interest rates?

The interview is over by the time we arrive in Marrickville. Albanese's house is full of cops, but the elusive muse Toto is nowhere to be seen. My brain is in overdrive. I'm war gaming a structure for the campaign essay, the RBA decision is bearing down, I'm trying to work out how I can surreptitiously watch the Lowe press conference while Toto is procured for Bowers' camera. Albanese tracks down his son, Nathan, who has the dog at his mother's place. There's some discussion about how to get Toto back. I'm nervous about getting this commentary done. I'm also anxious about being in Albanese's house; he's tired and I don't want to intrude. Where's the dog? Do we need the dog? Should I head back to the city?

Albanese watches me standing in his living room racked with relentless, unavoidable calculations. He picks up the TV remote and turns on one of the news channels. He points at the lounge. Grateful, I sit. There is an overwhelming noise at the front of the house and the sound of skidding on floorboards. Toto is home, flying down the hallway, overcome by the sight of her master. A joyful reunion ensues. Bowers gets his pictures and I get the RBA governor.

Philip Lowe calling time on the era of free money feels epochal; certainly bigger than the contest we are currently in. But Albanese isn't watching. I'm in such a frenzy it takes me a few minutes to notice this. He's wandered off through the back room, towards the yard, nudging a ball for Toto. The only unoccupied segment of my brain is confused. Am I preventing him from watching something he should be watching? This detachment – it's nuts, right?

Lowe's press conference ebbs, then we roll straight into a presser with Scott Morrison and Josh Frydenberg. *Have you just lost the campaign?* is the first question. Morrison frowns. "Of course not," the prime minister says. Frydenberg – who has the worst poker face I've seen in politics – is flushed with the exertion of looking unperturbed.

In Marrickville, Albanese is less combatant, more breeze, wafting through his place of retreat, curling out a door, rising into the sunlight, with a delirious dog yapping down below. I can imagine the scene back in the city right now: the strategists and staffers crowded around the televisions in Labor's campaign headquarters, watching intently, parsing every word, drafting the lines, praying this reversal is a sign from God – so why is Albanese powered down, throwing a ball to a dog?

Months later, during one of our conversations for this essay, Albanese is tethered by the weight of the office and hermetically sealed in his Parliament House suite. He's sitting behind the desk. His chosen art, a milky yellow Lloyd Rees landscape, hangs on the wall, his books are on the shelves, and a crush of advisers desperate for his attention queues outside the door.

I ask him whether he remembers that day in the campaign, the rate hike day. "Sure," he says.

"Why did you check out and play with Toto? Why not watch what was happening? It was pretty important."

Australia's thirty-first prime minister looks at me with pity. Possibly encouragement. A look a parent would give a clueless child before engaging an after-school tutor and a life coach.

"I thought in advance they'd increase rates," Albanese says. "I don't think that day was a decisive factor in the campaign."

Mentally, Albanese was already where instinct told him the campaign story would end. With him in the Lodge. Unnecessary diversions or exertions drain energy. Clear the clutter. Focus on future tense. You never win the war if you get bogged down in the wrong battle.

"I never thought it was certain, but I thought we'd win."

The unbearable lightness of being

Anthony Albanese intuits as much as he plans and calculates. He's a gut-instinct politician. Everybody who knows him says this. While his backroom advisers and his more technocratic, policy-obsessed colleagues put together PowerPoints and flow charts and strategy documents, weighted by facts and counterfactuals, Albanese is often cartwheeling several steps in front, light as a tumbleweed.

When he fronted the voters shortly after Scott Morrison called the election on 10 April, Albanese was armed with a script the brains trust had prepared for the opening salvo of the campaign. The opening call to action had been honed down to the semi-colons, as these things always are, because the initial framing of the contest matters. Think about John Howard opening the 2004 election contest asking voters who they trusted to manage the economy and national security. A trust pitch from late-term Howard was about as audacious as it comes, but it proved the winning overture when the opponent was Mark Latham. That question framed the battle. But in 2022, Albanese threw out his script and winged it. The result was in no way memorable.

After the long struggle to reach the top of Labor politics, after a lifetime of making his own luck, Albanese couldn't visualise a situation where he wasn't battle-ready. He didn't listen when people who cared about him said, *you can't know what it's like to survive a campaign until you've stood at the apex of one. Read your bloody briefing pack. Do your homework.* The prime minister has deep belief in his own strategic judgment, and that conviction gets reinforced because on the big political calls Albanese is mostly right. Often, but not always, because only deities have perfect judgment. Voters didn't notice the Labor leader's day-one campaign improvisation. It was suboptimal but innocuous. But day two of winging it was hard to miss. Albanese had opened the contest in expansive spirits, believing the voters wanted a conversation, as opposed to imbibing talking points on wash, rinse, repeat. He was probably right about that, but the travelling press pack arrayed between a putative prime minister and the public was in a febrile flex. Albanese failed the day-two pop quiz: what was the official cash rate? What was the unemployment rate?

Some voters were destabilised by the brain fade. The baby-faced assassins of the press gallery got high on the pursuit, forgetting that the only cohort people despise more than politicians are preening journalists. The inquisition from the fourth estate got worse, as Albanese fluffed various iterations of Trivial Pursuit as the campaign dragged on. The drive-by aggression probably helped him. But that opening lapse by Albanese wasn't unimportant. In a way it was revelatory, because it showed he wasn't entirely prepared. When I say he was unprepared, I mean unprepared for the unavoidable prelude to government: the campaign.

This lack of preparation revealed the candidate was running several steps in front. Albanese was expanding, thinking (and saying) he would answer every journalist's question. He was already in dialogue with the Australian people, which is a post-victory status. Albanese fell to earth: you can't get to round three without surviving round one. Campaigns aren't a conversation, and they certainly aren't coronations. Campaigns are message wars mediated by an incurious, deadening apparatus intent on seeking heat, not light. The media will happily knock you flat, because the only thing better than a nightly gaffe leading the 6 p.m. news is a comeback story by the close of the campaign. Australians love a comeback story and in the digital age, where hyperventilation drives audience engagement, which drives clicks and shares and who knows how many TikTok memes, politics and reality television are sometimes indistinguishable.

Albanese's lightness is a signature. This man can dance between raindrops. If we think back to the days of *Rats in the Ranks*, a documentary about internecine politics in Sydney's inner west, Albanese was able to play a starring role while remaining entirely off-camera. One of his long-time friends, Meredith Burgmann, feminist, activist and former president of the NSW Legislative Council, says Albanese once gave her a critical bit of advice. "I was fighting a particularly awful preselection thing, and he just said – you've got to keep them dancing. At the time I had no idea what he meant by that, but now I do. What he meant was they can't see you as having no further moves. You've got to keep them dancing." Election campaigns nail a choreographer's feet to the earth, and Labor leaders always face tougher scrutiny because, in the main, Rupert Murdoch and the editors who live to please him would sooner see a camel pass through the eye of a needle than a progressive in the Lodge.

Lightness is one of those attributes: sometimes help, sometimes hindrance. Albanese's lightness revealed he wasn't protected by numbing layers of calluses and scar tissue built up during three years of Opposition. The pandemic had disrupted politics. The biggest public health crisis in a century had required representative democracy to be more than a spectacle of pulverising, naysaying partisan politics. He wasn't entirely battle-ready because he hadn't done three years of town halls where at least half of the fifty people who turn up are there on the misapprehension that you are Scott Morrison, or the state premier. He hadn't done the grinding in the parliament, with the associated intra-day arbitrary media flagellation, because parliament didn't sit as often, and when it did, it had to attend to saving lives and livelihoods, not furnishing training opportunities for alternative prime ministers.

Albanese is a savant about numbers because he's had to build his own political machine. He didn't arrive with a trade union base. He's had to count every advance, every vote, maintaining a meticulous ledger in his head. If you have numbers, you win; if you don't, you lose. A number falling right out of his head on day two of the contest jolted him, and it jolted the campaign. Penny Wong says the early campaign stumbles were an existential crossroads. "You either step up, or we are all dead," Wong says. "Anthony knew that. You don't go through that kind of experience without finding more in yourself."

But Wong says victory wasn't all on the leader. Winning or losing wasn't "just about him, it's the architecture of the group who were pulling for him." The team rallied. Albanese was reminded of the lesson he'd absorbed in stages over the previous three years: winning takes your intuition, but it also takes a village, with PowerPoints and spreadsheets. Use us. Let us help.

Albanese needs this prompt periodically, not because he's particularly arrogant but because he's self-made. He's not used to having a trailing support crew to bail him out. He's not from the upper middle class. He wasn't raised with the expectation of a network to open doors and magic away problems. Getting by or sinking without a trace – that responsibility has been all on him. That can make a person solitary. It can make a person default to dreaming and strategising and periodically running right off the rails in their own head.

If you want to understand Albanese – who he is, how he functions, what he will do with power, how he will lead, how he will work with the progressive parliament Australians elected on 21 May, what we know about him, and what we are yet to learn – there's only one place to start.

At the beginning.

CAMPERDOWN

Australia's thirty-first prime minister can't remember a time when life hasn't required him to think three steps ahead. His mother, Maryanne, was often unwell, and from the time he was born in 1963, it was just the two of them in a council house in Sydney's inner west. He wouldn't meet his father, Carlo, until he was an adult.

When Maryanne was incapacitated, young Anthony was in loco parentis. He did the finances, paid the rent and the household bills. When he was twelve, he got himself a paper round. After school, Albanese sold copies of The Sun and The Daily Mirror on Bligh Street, amid peak-hour traffic. He chose that location because the kids got $16 a week instead of $12.

Maryanne had rheumatoid arthritis. Management of her chronic pain was sporadic and ineffectual until a mate from university, Mark Jones, came around for dinner one night and saw Anthony having to cut up his mother's food so she could eat. Albanese recounts this experience a lot, because humans curate our biographies. The stories we share from our past are often didactic, and this particular anecdote explains how he came to understand the value of accruing a network.

Mark was from Hunters Hill and his mother worked as a receptionist for David Champion, a medical specialist and surgeon. "As a result of that connection, I got her an appointment," Albanese says. "Dr Champion restructured her hands and feet – long operations. Two different times at Sydney Hospital in Macquarie Street. She was in there and did months of rehab. It meant she could walk without acute pain, she could use her hands much more and was in a better state than she was fifteen years earlier." Maryanne used to tell Anthony it's not what you know, it's who you know, and that transformative experience lingers in her son's consciousness.

Before that, things had been rough. "One time she was in a small hospital in Glebe," he recalls. "It was an old building. Mum was upstairs and due to be discharged. On the way out, as they put the bed down the stairs she slid off the bed, basically down the stairs in this hospital." Albanese was fourteen or fifteen when he witnessed his mother being treated as an inconvenience. "They picked her up, put her in the ambulance because they needed the bed. I was like, are you kidding me? I was the only one at home and I had to look after her."

When Maryanne was prescribed the corticosteroid prednisone as part of earlier treatment for the arthritis, things went awry, and young Anthony again had to try to sort it out. "I remember having an argument with the doctor as a school student," Albanese says. "Are you waiting for her to die? She was on the wrong dose, things were going wrong, and they weren't doing anything to fix it. She lost control over her nervous system, she lost her speech, she was shaking the whole time, she was incredibly emotional and frustrated by it all, and they weren't doing anything to change things."

The indignity of these experiences made him angry. Adolescent Anthony was a bull in a china shop, trying to crash through hard barriers by force of personality and will. He was devoted to his mother. Their bond was unshakeable. Maryanne was the centre of his world, and the gap between her generosity of spirit and the indifference of the systems they interacted with felt intolerable.

But he was also a kid, forced to be an adult. If you've had this experience, you'll know how visceral it is to oscillate between deep insecurity and intrusive practical responsibility. Periodically, that pressure stoked resentment. He acted out. He was sometimes naughty at school and got into fights after the bell rang. "Now, they'd call the parents. But back then, it was no big deal." Albanese was rebellious. He took risks. "There were all sorts of things we did to get by," he says, without further elaboration. He was perceived by others as a "pretty tough kid." He laughs. "There would be people [from back then] who would be quite surprised now that I'm sitting in the prime minister's office," Albanese says. "To say the least."

Albanese is a life learner. People and place are his anchors. A lot of people who have struggled in childhood need distance from those experiences. They need to be something else. They pull up roots and begin again elsewhere, but Albanese has remained in the neighbourhood where he grew to adulthood. He has gentrified as Albo country has gentrified. A childhood in a council house is another country once you inhabit the most powerful office in Australia. Albanese has overt power, creature comforts. He walks on plush carpet and sits on bespoke furniture. Someone brings him coffee when his energy flags. There's a cook at the residences to take care of meals. Toto can hitch a ride on the air-force plane and chase a ball down the rolling lawn at Kirribilli that slopes to Sydney Harbour. We're not in Camperdown anymore. He's not the kid who had to wonder when Mum would come home from hospital and what condition she would be in by the time she returned; whether he'd have to help her into the shower or watch her bump down stairs on her backside because she couldn't stand up on crippled feet.

But at some level, you are always that kid. Camperdown set Albanese's character. Many of the prime minister's core survival skills formed there. Politicians are conditioned by the job to be selfish and dictatorial, so as a cohort, they aren't particularly self-aware. You can't tell them anything. They already know all the things. But he tries to be self-aware about the impact of childhood conditioning. Albanese says he's totally self-reliant. "I don't like to be needed. That's a direct product of [my] history." His mother needed him, and he needed her. His country needs him, and he is a person who needs purpose. It's odd, given that, to want to pull off the yoke, but Albanese's observation is honest. Obligation is duty, and duty is weight, and weight impedes flight.

Even though he has staff to organise his life, Albanese seeks to control his own environment. "I'll do things in the office that can create problems. I do stuff in my diary, I organise meetings. I do stuff, you know, that's me" – meaning he initiates things without necessarily consulting others. He also gathers people around him who know what he needs. A number of people working for him now have been with him or adjacent to him since the 1980s. He doesn't have to be verbal about what he needs, because Albo people already know; they are experts in the ebbs and flows of his personality. They can read the moods, like weather forecasters.

Today, the boss is cloudy with a chance of an evening thunderstorm. Experienced staff intuit what can be shaped and what has to play out. Political offices often have factions and intrigues. Albanese's office is no exception. People can move in and out of favour for unfathomable reasons. Staffing can be a feudal and toxic business. But Albo people also tend to exhibit a form of platonic devotion that eclipses any transient homicidal impulses. Politics is war. War breeds intimacy and camaraderie. It's what sustains souls in adverse environments.

As well as tending his own minutiae, Albanese also needs to keep moving. He finds it difficult to defer tasks that can be transacted quickly. He points at his in and out trays on his desk in the prime ministerial office. They are sparse. "There is nothing in my signing pile," he says. "I never do anything tomorrow that I can do today." Working through tasks requires a measure of anticipation. "If I do this, then what happens? I've thought that through. For some people, if there's a problem or an issue, they don't think through to the next step."

"I had to plan," he says. "If I didn't plan, my mum wouldn't have food, we wouldn't pay rent." Even now, Albanese remains attentive to his material needs, preparing for all contingencies. "I've never run out of anything at home," he says. I'm incredulous. Never? Come on. With a lifestyle as busy as yours? "Never," Albanese insists. "Milk. Frozen food. Coffee. Toilet paper. Food for Toto. Here's another example. I've never paid a cent in interest on a credit card. I pay bills before they are due even though that's not an economically rational thing to do."

Albanese's friend and key factional ally Mark Butler, now Australia's health minister, says the prime minister's habitual self-reliance is "a hard-wired thing, almost subconscious." Butler believes it's a survival skill. It's muscle memory. And it's the bedrock of his strategic capability. "A lot of us have fluid backgrounds – different family circumstances that shift and change over the course of our adolescence," Butler says. "I don't have a single childhood experience; it was a series of changing experiences. Anthony's was a much more ..." he pauses briefly. "He had a very defined experience as a child and adolescent, and I think it shaped him. It's not as natural for him to bring people around him as it is for others."

Meredith Burgmann believes Albanese's strategic nous stems from "bringing himself up." He learnt at a young age to play three-dimensional chess. "It took me a while because I'm not into the internecine stuff, but I did come to realise in time how very good at strategy he is," she says. "After a while it got to the point where I wouldn't make a significant political move without talking to him first."

She also believes the influence of Tom Uren – a giant of left politics, a former deputy leader of the ALP and a father figure to Albanese – added valuable inflection points. Albanese worked as an adviser to Uren on the road to federal politics. Uren was a remarkable Australian – a professional boxer in his youth, a prisoner of war who worked on the notorious Burma Railway before being transferred to Japan, where he witnessed the atomic bombing of Nagasaki. Burgmann says Uren taught him about "forgiveness and long-term thinking." Another old friend, Paul Murphy, who has known Albanese since 1983, says Uren impressed on his protégé the need in politics and in life to find people of goodwill wherever they are. To find a way to work with them to achieve change. "That's something he's really taken to heart and lived," Murphy says. "It's only natural that when you are younger you are much more bull at a gate, but he really has learnt patience. That capacity to find people and deal with people in different ways to achieve things."

If Albanese's childhood was a rolling seminar in class consciousness, Labor politics offered a productive outlet for his prodigious energy. He joined Young Labor while he was still in high school, and he helped revive the Labor club when he went to Sydney University. He was the first in his family to enter tertiary education. Years of frustration were channelled into political organising, and young Albanese (or "old Albo" as some of the colleagues prefer, meaning the beta version) wasn't inclined to take prisoners.

Catherine Cusack studied economics at Sydney University at the same time as Albanese. She was the president of the Young Liberals when Albanese, a noisy young inner-city activist, was blazing a trail through student politics. Cusack is a great admirer of the prime minister now. But at that time, in the mid-1980s, she didn't know him personally. She was apprehensive about the young left-wing "firebrand." In those days he was Hard Left. She recalls Albanese "missiles" fired in correspondence – ideological screeds laced with ad hominem arrived typewritten, with hand corrections. The Young Liberals, including the president, were capitalist pigs, or words to that effect; the tone was "very left-wing, very dogmatic, very aggressive."

Cusack says Albanese attempted to challenge her to a public debate. Bob Hawke was in power and had launched the priority one jobs program for unemployed youth – a significant controversy on campus at that time. "The first letter I got, I didn't know how to answer and I certainly didn't want to be debating him," Cusack laughs. "It's hilarious to look back on it. I tried not to tell anyone about it because I was terrified someone would say to me, 'Go get him, Catherine'. I certainly didn't want to be in that situation." Cusack didn't reply to the first letter. A few weeks later Albanese dispatched a second letter, declaring she was a coward for not responding and offering her another chance to debate. "I didn't reply to the second letter and thank goodness he stopped writing," she laughs.

Uren says in his memoir *Straight Left* that when he brought Albanese on to his ministerial staff, some comrades in the Left faction expressed horror. "Oh, you are putting a young Trot on your staff." (For the record, Uren disagreed with the characterisation, and predicted Albanese would lead the Left, then the Labor Party.) Burgmann says young Anthony had "no second gear." She says if he wanted to beat someone in an argument, "he could really go into it. He and I had terrible arguments. We'd end up both of us crying. It was because he felt strongly about things."

It wasn't all anger. Some of it was unconfined joy. "He was great fun," Burgmann says. "You always felt the party started when Albo arrived. When he wanted to, he could be very charismatic even. He knew how to get people to do stuff because they wanted to be doing stuff with him. Paul Murphy reinforces the portrait of a young extrovert. "We were both serious young insects, but we had a lot of fun," he says. "We bonded over a shared love of music, different bands, football – although I don't share his passion for the Rabbitohs." Murphy says he and Albanese spent a decent portion of their youth "shit-talking each other over a game of pool."

Albanese has the measure of ruthlessness that politics requires. But he is also loyal in a transactional business, so he has allies and proper friends, including in places you'd never expect. He cultivates people, and invests in long relationships. He's tough, and wily, and calculating. But he can also be kind, often at just the right moment.

He feels things. Voters would have clocked this dimension of the prime minister by now. The lip quivers. He brims. Sometimes the feelings over-flow. That's not affectation or a performance. It's a core attribute. He wants to keep himself open to the world. Empathy in politics, if you can main-tain it, works as a sixth sense. It helps him anticipate. A lot of leaders are natural pessimists, because assuming the worst saves time and energy, but Albanese assumes you are for him until he learns you are against him, and then it's war. There are intimates, allies, and then there are enemies. Often, he'll seek to neutralise rivals, and politics furnishes a number of options for achieving that. If enemies can't be disarmed, he escalates to exclusion.

While he accrues connections with relentless focus, the flipside is his need for personal space. He prioritises thinking time so he can ponder various actions and reactions. If he can't retreat from noise, he'll screen it out even if this inconveniences others. When he was young, and had saved up enough money to travel, he went overseas by himself for six months. Albanese was social, met up with people along the way, but he didn't want to move in a pack. These instincts carry over into contemporary life. He retreats, but when alone he'll connect with his network on his terms. I've lost count of the number of times I've gone downstairs from the press gal-lery to interview politicians from across the political spectrum and they've just got off the phone with Albanese.

When he won the seat of Grayndler and began the federal politician's fly-in, fly-out lifestyle, the decades of having two lives – one in Sydney's inner west and another in Canberra – his equilibrium wasn't disturbed at all, although he acknowledges his former wife, Carmel, wasn't happy with a divided existence towards the end of their marriage. Arriving in Canberra in 1996, Albanese began in a group house, then bought a flat near the parliament by himself because he needed a private space to retreat to. "Even the journey I'm on now," he says, meaning the journey to becoming prime minister of Australia, "some people, I think, would find it really lonely. They'd have great difficulty with that. I'm okay. Last night I sat at the Lodge by myself, watched the footy, had a beer. I'm fine with that."

Butler has known Albanese since he was the state secretary of the Federated Miscellaneous Workers Union in South Australia. He says the prime minister isn't one or two things, he's a whole range of things, and some of his qualities are contradictory. Fighter. Life of the party. Lone wolf. Networker. Consensus-builder. "This is counterintuitive for a lot of people, because he's a fighter and he's had to fight to get to where he is," Butler says. "He's not one or the other. He's genuinely both.

"I think he's agile and he can adapt to circumstances. When he needs to fight, he fights; he's as good as anyone I've seen. He's relentless, he's got good instincts, he's tactically clever, courageous, good on the stump, has a network to draw on like no one else – certainly no one in our party."

"But I think there's two phases to Anthony's life: one is getting to the point of power and influence and getting things done, and the second is how he uses it."

Getting to the point of power and influence wasn't achieved by a charm offensive, although Albanese has mastered the empathetic politician's art of active listening and mirroring. Mastery of machine and parliamentary politics is a game of snakes and ladders, sequences of advances and reversals. Albanese's ascent in politics, from the youth wing to the prime ministership, has been about numbers, strategy, networks and, in periods of battle, brute force.

In Labor politics, some leaders are anointed. They are either marked for greatness in the court of their peers or cultivate a sense of inexorability about themselves until the prophecy becomes self-fulfilling. Albanese isn't from this cohort. He's been an insurgent and a bomb-thrower for most of his professional life. Understanding this modus operandi and mindset is critical to understanding Australia's thirty-first prime minister. Apart from the opportunity to work for Uren, a backroom apprenticeship that was created for him by elders in the Labor Left for pragmatic reasons – to give the hot-headed inner-city activist some male mentorship to make sure he didn't explode like a firecracker – Albanese has had to blast his way in.

Back in the 1980s in Sydney, before he made the transition to federal politics at the start of the Howard era, it was man against machine. Albanese was an agitator and organiser pitted against the Labor leadership at Sussex Street. The Right faction were the kings and kingmakers, and essential to this hegemony was a mantra of "divide and conquer the Left." The Left in New South Wales was split and Albanese, moving through the youth wing to the state organisation, was a minority, minority player. He was aligned with the minority Hard Left group in the minority Left faction.

In New South Wales, the cleave was Soft Left and Hard Left. In a paper about factionalism published in the *Australian Journal of Political Science*, then Labor staffer, now economics professor and Labor frontbencher Andrew Leigh says the NSW Hard Left of this era differentiated itself from the Soft Left through its preoccupation with union participation in party fora and with international issues. Elements of the subfaction in New South Wales were hostile to the neoliberal economics of Bob Hawke and Paul Keating, and also "maintained closer links with broader left-wing groups, such as the Communist Party of Australia, People for Nuclear Disarmament and the African National Congress" – although Leigh points out that some of the differences were grounded in personality as much as in ideology.

It was an era of fierce combat. Albanese moved through rolling internecine battles from being president of NSW Young Labor to assistant general secretary of the NSW branch of Labor in 1989, replacing John Faulkner, who was bound for the Senate. When he worked at Sussex Street, he was alone – one left-winger in an office of twenty. Reflecting on that period, Albanese says as assistant secretary, "I never ever had the numbers for anything – state conference, admin committee, national conference." Thinking two steps ahead was crucial to professional survival. "Anything I did, I had to think about what's the reaction and what's the next battle, and I was pretty successful," he says. Many people in those circumstances would have felt isolated, but Albanese prospered as a lone wolf. "Some people would have found that incredibly difficult," he says.

Acts of aggression between the Right and the Left and between the warring Left groups ranged between dangerous and puerile. One anecdote from the latter category: at some point in his tenure at Sussex Street, Right faction colleagues moved Albanese's office without consulting him while he was on a study trip to the United States, then changed the locks so he couldn't access the space. A posse of supporters, including Burgmann, who brought power tools to the party office, took the territory back.

The Soft Left was led by the Ferguson brothers, Martin and Laurie. Martin Ferguson was the general secretary of the Federated Miscellaneous Workers Union, known as the "Missos", by the mid-1980s and rising through the union hierarchy. The Fergusons were dynastic Labor players. Their father, Jack Ferguson, had been deputy premier of the state from 1976 to 1983. The Left split was inflamed by events that followed Ferguson senior's resignation in September 1983. "We were in dispute with the Ferguson forces in the mid-1980s," Burgmann says. She says she was concerned at various times that rhetorical arguments between the groups could escalate into physical violence. "It was full-on, it was nasty."

While the Ferguson Soft Left was aligned with the "Missos," the Hard Left in New South Wales was aligned with the metal workers' union. During the 1960s, the metals were more connected to the Communist Party of Australia than Labor. But during subsequent decades, the AMWU became the largest left-affiliated Labor union. While contemporary Albanese is more known for his pragmatism than his ideological motivations, Burgmann says Albanese and the group he built maintained a broader sense of left politics and left causes. "We were the left that had come to the Labor Party to advance left causes," she says. Identity didn't begin and end with the ALP. "Often, he and I would be the only people speaking at a broad left conference because we actually believed in progressive politics generally. He was alert to the problems of just being involved in the Labor Party."

Burgmann says Albanese would distinguish their group from the Fergusons, by saying, "The Fergusons are in the left because they are in the Labor Party, and we are in the Labor Party because we are in the left. What he was trying to say was that our side – the union-based, Frank Walker group – were part of the general left and pursued left activity inside Labor, whereas the Fergusons were in the Labor Party, looked at the Right faction and thought no, they are too terrible, so they became the left."

But she says he was always practical in his outlook: "He realised very early on that being left-wing was not something that you did to make you feel better, you had to actually get stuff done." Albanese views the Labor Party "as a strategic way to progress left policies – which would be his main criticism of the Greens. The policies are similar, but they are pursued by complaining and campaigning, whereas we are more interested in results. He's always been really focused on results."

Given his commitment to the broader political left, and the circles he moved in – young Gramsci-reading idealists preoccupied with international solidarity movements – Albanese could easily have skewed even harder left. Burgmann says that didn't happen largely because of his upbringing – his beloved and staunchly Labor-voting mother, and the practical sensibilities of Camperdown. "That part of the inner city was still very Labor," she says. Communist philosophy might be appealing, but Albanese isn't motivated by theory. Younger Albanese was always Hard Left, "but he was never dopey about it. I suspect, from time to time, I was quite dopey about it, but he was always focused on getting something done. There's no point in being right if you can never get it to happen."

By 1990, Martin Ferguson was ACTU president – a stepping stone to the federal arena. Ferguson and Albanese arrived in federal politics in the same year: 1996. Albanese alighted in Canberra with a reputation as a tough inner-city activist and factional powerbroker. He enjoyed throwing rhetorical bombs at John Howard during his opening years in Canberra. By the time his second term rolled around, the ambitious up-and-comer wanted to advance to the front bench. But Ferguson wasn't having that. Ferguson had his own ticket for the shadow ministry and was powerful enough internally to head Albanese and his group off at the pass. "When I got here, I couldn't get elected to the front bench," Albanese says. "That was the structure. I couldn't get through despite having support from the leader, Kim Beazley, and the leader in the Senate, John Faulkner."

By 1996, Mark Butler was an emerging power player in South Australia. He'd been a student activist while studying law at the University of Adelaide and had risen to state secretary of the "Missos." Butler encountered Albanese shortly after that elevation. He remembers being at the National Press Club in Canberra on the night in 1998 when Albanese's front bench aspiration was thwarted by Ferguson. Albanese did his block. Butler remembers the explosion. But as the saying goes, don't get mad, get even.

By 2007, Butler was in the federal parliament. He says "at some point" Albanese approached him about bringing the two Lefts together. "Anthony said, this is ridiculous, we are going to have to stop it – when you are ready to come and talk, come and talk." Butler says factional détente wasn't achieved in a single moment. "We became closer and started to cooperate more." This redux in the power dynamics in the left was highly significant. Albanese moved from the minority group in the minority faction to being in command of the left. It cost Butler his relationship with the Fergusons, but it handed Butler and Albanese much greater control of the federal caucus. "Anthony recognised it was self-defeating to keep fighting," Butler says. "From the time I arrived, it felt like we could get things done sensibly."

This power-sharing agreement created stability and space for Albanese to develop a different modus operandi in public life. He went from insurgent to establishment. During this period, Albanese was a counsellor to two prime ministers.

While his long guerrilla campaign was in hiatus during the Rudd/Gillard period, some of the outsider habits and mindset persisted. With Labor back in power after 2007, Albanese led government business in the House. He collaborated with colleagues, but, institutionally, managing House business is a sanctioned fiefdom. If you are competent, you are left to your own devices. As well as the duties in the House, Albanese held a key ministry: infrastructure. He was in the cabinet, part of the economic engine room of the government, but his portfolio allowed a high degree of autonomy and that suited his instincts.

During the first iteration of Kevin Rudd, Albanese was an important player, but he was not in the inner sanctum – the "gang of four" (Rudd, Julia Gillard, Wayne Swan and Lindsay Tanner). Colleagues say Albanese was shocked when the frustrations with Rudd escalated into a full-blown leadership challenge in June 2010. He wasn't the only one. That night looms very large in my memory mainly because of the chaos. Unlike all the leadership coups that have followed the Rudd ousting, there wasn't an elaborately choreographed crescendo. Much of the government had no idea that some colleagues were intent on blasting Rudd out of the prime ministership until the story broke on the ABC television news on the night of 23 June. As Gillard has said subsequently of those events, there was nothing to see with that leadership challenge until such time as there was everything to see.

Albanese believed the 2010 insurrection would kill the government and destroy not one but two Labor prime ministers – a cut-through political judgment that several colleagues seemed to lack in the heat of the moment. Given surprises in politics, like unexpected leadership coups, are rarely welcome, henceforth Albanese kept an even closer eye on the caucus. Albanese remained the key parliamentary tactician during the Gillard prime ministership, keeping Labor's legislative program on track during the minority parliament that followed the 2010 election.

This required Albanese to develop relationships of trust with crossbenchers. Trust was the glue of the transactions. One of the kingmakers, Tony Windsor, began the forty-third parliament thinking Albanese was a "smart arse, a student-politics type." But his view changed. Windsor watched Albanese – a Rudd person – work around the clock to deliver Gillard's agenda. "No one worked harder for Julia than him," he told me in 2021. Windsor learnt to trust Albanese, who worked amiably with the crossbench while other Labor colleagues "seethed" about the constraints of minority government. "Albanese took it in his stride. I found him very good to work with. I never felt shafted, and you can't say that about too many people in politics."

The pulverising negativity of that period also cemented a significant friendship between Albanese and another wily factional veteran, the manager of Opposition business, Christopher Pyne. While Tony Abbott lobbed rhetorical bombs at Gillard in the chamber, Pyne engaged in off-the-books shuttle diplomacy with Albanese. Pyne says of that period: "We used to spend quite a lot of time with each other, making room for one another's requirements without blowing up politics in Australia, and we came to realise we were both pretty straightforward characters and our word was our bond. If we said we were going to do something, we did it."

Maintaining the confidence of so many actors in the parliament helped Albanese to keep the goodwill of both Gillard and Rudd at a time when Labor's civil war was forcing colleagues to pick a side and express their allegiance tribally. The professional and personal adversity of that parliament burned out and traumatised many of Albanese's contemporaries. But his talent for dexterity, fluidity and strategic ambiguity served everybody's interests during this period, including his own. The skills Albanese honed – maintaining lines of communication, tending a diverse set of relationships without getting caught in the crosshairs, understanding some of what nonaligned political actors need in order to be cooperative – ultimately set him up for leadership in the forty-seventh parliament.

Not all the judgments between 2010 and 2013 were perfect by any stretch. Albanese's brokering of the deal to appoint the Liberal Peter Slipper as speaker was a bad call. But Albanese's energy, resilience and adaptability were also a wellspring powering the Rudd and Gillard governments.

While he managed to hold the regard of the two prime ministers, colleagues insist Albanese was always a rusted-on Rudd person, whether he owned that allegiance publicly or not. As Gillard notes in her memoir, *My Story*, "throughout my leadership, Albo supported Kevin." She had known Albanese since he was nineteen, and the two had enjoyed "a bantering friendship," but "from the moment I arrived in federal parliament, Albo and I were pitched against each other." When push came to shove, they were on opposite sides of the old Left split. Albanese was from the Hard Left and she was a Fergusonite who "toed the line" during her early years in politics.

Rudd ultimately returned to the leadership in June 2013. Some colleagues say Albanese was telegraphing support for a Rudd reboot at least twelve months before it happened, although he was very careful about what he said outside various closed circles of trust, given that holding that view would have rendered his position under Gillard untenable. Albanese eventually went public with his allegiance in a memorable press conference where he famously declared his preference for "fighting Tories" – not his Labor colleagues. Several frontbenchers quit when Gillard was rolled. Rudd promoted Albanese to deputy prime minister. As Rudd's deputy, it was official. Albanese had finally reached insider status, and his elevation by Rudd positioned him as a leader-in-waiting. For a time, he was in the "gang of three" with Rudd and Chris Bowen, the NSW right-winger and avowed Rudd backer who was given Treasury after Gillard was deposed.

Albanese had reached the inner inner-sanctum, but he was not yet the front man. Rudd went on to lose the 2013 election. After the defeat, Albanese stood for the Labor leadership and easily won the ALP's first grass-roots ballot. One of Rudd's bequests – designed as an automatic stabiliser against Canberra's emerging coup culture – was a historic rule change giving Labor members a direct say in the party leadership.

Albanese was the grassroots choice, but the Victorian right-winger Bill Shorten had a lock on the caucus. When it came to the caucus ballot, the Right faction backed their candidate to a man and woman, and a decisive handful of left-wingers in the caucus also chose Shorten over Albanese. While Albanese was the ascendant national Left powerbroker, decades of intra-factional conflict meant old enmities and allegiances ran deep.

Losing the opportunity to lead Labor was obviously a blow. Albanese would have thought he'd missed his chance. He reverted to insurgency. He wasn't overtly disloyal to Shorten (although disloyalty in politics is always an eye-of-the-beholder activity). Instead, Albanese went back to running his own race. This is a trivial example, but it speaks to Albanese's mindset. During the Shorten era, all media releases and transcripts from shadow ministers were supposed to be cleared through the leader's office. Albanese and his staff never complied with the practice. "Albo" maintained his status as an independent, self-governing municipality within Shorten Labor.

Albanese also took opportunities periodically to engage in product differentiation. There are two standout examples. In 2017, after a controversial Labor advertisement targeted at marginal seats surfaced, featuring Shorten promising to "build Australian first, buy Australian first and employ Australians first," a brief pile-on ensued about nativism and dog-whistling. Albanese promptly declared the campaign a "shocker." He also pointed out the advertisement had not been seen by the party's national executive. The advert was pulled.

Then in June 2018, Albanese used a significant speech to offer Labor a sliding doors moment. Strangely enough, this particular speech was cleared through the leader's office. Albanese used the Gough Whitlam Oration to implicitly criticise Shorten's political strategy and offer an alternative would-be prime ministerial tone: less partisan, more business-friendly, more sunny uplands, less scary revenue measures. Albanese warned Labor could not expect to "slide into government off the back of our opponent's failures." This adventurism had an undeclared context. Opinion polls were pointing to a Labor victory in 2019, but not everybody was convinced Shorten had the winning pitch. Camp Albanese were worried Shorten and the program might not get them there. But others wanted to stick with the incumbent. The sotto voce arguments from that time continue to influence relationships in Labor to this day.

The nervousness ultimately proved to be well founded, but the caucus declined the option of pursuing an alternative. Albanese's kite-flying went nowhere, Labor stuck with Shorten, and the shadow infrastructure minister stowed his ambition. While losing in 2019 was an agony for Labor and doubtless infuriating for Albanese, politics is a funny business. If Albanese had won the caucus ballot in 2013, or if he'd become leader in 2018, there is no guarantee he would have beaten either Malcolm Turnbull or Scott Morrison. It's entirely possible that getting the leadership early would have cruelled his chance of becoming prime minister.

After Shorten's defeat in 2019, it was time for Albanese to come in from the cold. Labor was shellshocked when Albanese took the party leadership after the election loss. Shorten had been Opposition leader for two terms. But Albanese, because of his age, would not be given that luxury.

One of Albanese's talents is the art of indeterminate age. For a long time, I assumed he and I were of the same vintage because we turned up at Parliament House at the same time. I got a shock when I learnt he was almost a decade older than me. His political brand has never been middle-aged suburban dad. He's "Albo" — a lover of live music, a drinker of hipster craft beers, DJ by request. But as the Melbourne political columnist Shaun

Carney has pointed out, Albanese was fifty-six when he took the leadership, making him the oldest first-time Opposition leader since Arthur Calwell became Labor leader aged sixty-three in 1960.

Albanese took the leadership unopposed. Labor was not turning to a slick saviour after the rout. The party was choosing an old dog for a hard road.

Taking the party leadership was both a beginning and an ending. Insurgency was done. New skills were required. Successful political leaders need sharp instincts and strategic brains. These qualities are necessary but ultimately insufficient. It's not enough to be right. Leadership is bringing people with you. It's about maintaining the architecture to deliver insight while preserving your authority.

Albanese knew how to win. He knew how to recruit people to a cause and to get them to a similar place. He'd been doing that since his teens. But to win, he had to learn to listen, to trust his team and to lead, understanding that sometimes leadership involves holding back rather than imagining it's all on you.

Albanese had the leadership, and for a while Labor found itself back in the contest. Morrison facilitated that by bumbling while large swathes of Australia burned at the end of 2019 and the beginning of 2020 – a catastrophe that demonstrated the reality of the climate crisis the Coalition had spent a decade denying. During that time, Australians saw the elements of the Morrison character that ultimately destroyed his prime ministership: a seeming inability to be the serious person serious times required; and a strange, aggressive passivity that swirled like a black hole at the centre of his rampant politicking.

After the fires, the coronavirus reached our shores, heralding disaster and disruption for the world. But Covid-19 was a temporary life raft for the Morrison prime ministership. Morrison learnt from the fires and grabbed that second crisis with both hands. He and the premiers formed a bipartisan war cabinet, and Albanese and Labor were blasted off the political map. Plague year 2020 was the worst of times for the Opposition.

During one of our conversations for this essay, Albanese, who came of age in the dense inner west of Sydney, kilometres from the cooling ocean breeze in the east, says he took to thinking about the surf.

"It's like you are in the surf, and you are enjoying it, but all of a sudden there's a wave that is much bigger than what you expected, and it's coming at you, and you can look at it, and struggle against it and get pummelled, or you can just dive down deep, watch the wave go over you, and come up for air, and wait for the right wave to come in," he says.

The year 2020 was one long dive. Albanese tells the story with his hands. "If you come up in the middle of the surf, you go ..." He makes a frenetic rolling motion with his hands. Dumped. Winded. Disorientated. "I was always very confident of what we were doing," he says. "But I think some in the show were frustrated that the wave was there."

Frustrated is right. Albanese was determined to be as constructive as possible during the pandemic, even if that meant disappearing from the public consciousness. His view was support what you can and oppose (or offer an alternative) when you must. Two judgments informed Albanese's strategy, one substantive, the other political. Covid-19 was serious. Lives and livelihoods were on the line. And his political judgment was that Australians would punish attention-seeking Opposition leaders obstructing opportunistically to keep themselves on the nightly news. This judgment proved to be correct.

But some Labor supporters, wounded by the 2019 loss, felt cut adrift by the strategy. Aggressive negativity against a loathed figure like Morrison was a comfort, a ritual, a morale boost. Shorten had been pugnacious with Abbott, Turnbull and Morrison. Albanese's dive-under-the-wave strategy was a distinct change of pace. While supporters fretted, colleagues were on board. If anyone had serious doubts about the new tone, they didn't verbalise them. But some believed Albanese had a bigger professional transition to make as Labor leader than the leader realised.

It had been a dislocating couple of years. In 2019, Albanese suffered a more profound blow than losing an election. His marriage ended. The end of his relationship with Carmel Tebbutt – the mother of his son, Nathan, his professional confidant and his life companion for thirty years – rocked Albanese to the core. He was walking around with open wounds. It took time to glue himself back together.

Albanese rolled from a profound personal crisis through a sequence of professional twists and turns: an election loss, taking the leadership, the political fillip of the bushfires, then making peace with temporary obscurity during the opening months of Covid. Even if you watched him closely during this period, as I was able to do, it wasn't clear during 2020 whether he was setting himself up for being Labor's nightwatchman – an honourable defeat in 2022, followed by a smooth handover of the party leadership to the next generation – or whether he was crouching, gathering energy, ready to go for Morrison's jugular.

His colleagues' internal angst reached a peak shortly after the Eden-Monaro by-election in July 2020. The by-election in the marginal electorate was triggered by the departure of Labor MP Mike Kelly, a respected former military officer and lawyer. This was a blow. Kelly was a substantial figure who liked to joke that he held the bellwether seat because he was related to half the Bega Valley. Given how Morrison was travelling, and the rally-around-incumbents dynamic of the pandemic, the timing stank.

Kelly had another candidate in mind to replace him, but Albanese grabbed Kristy McBain, a mayor of Bega. He had recruited her for the fight during a conversation at Merimbula Airport earlier in 2020. McBain ran an impeccable campaign and Albanese worked hard, as did the strategist who would spearhead the 2022 federal election, Paul Erickson. Labor held the seat.

This was an important test to pass, and Albanese was ebullient. Some of his colleagues feared too ebullient. The concern was that Albanese was visualising a universe where Labor romped into government in 2022 with seventy-six McBains. This wasn't realistic, and some voter perceptions about the leader playing back through research weren't encouraging.

About a month after the by-election, a group of senior colleagues staged an intervention. The conversation involved Albanese's inner circle: his two closest confidants, Penny Wong and Mark Butler; Labor's deputy leader Richard Marles; Albanese's chief of staff Tim Gartrell; and one member of the outer inner circle, Chris Bowen, the NSW right-winger and fellow member of the short-lived "gang of three" in the Rudd reboot. The conversation started out as a catch-up about the pandemic − Bowen at that time was the shadow health minister − but morphed into something else. The message from the high-powered group to Albanese was constructive and friendly, but it was also simple and direct: if the federal election was held today, we think we would lose. Right now, as things stand, you are not going to get there. But we can win, and here's some things that need to happen. You need to be sharper and your message needs to be clearer. Your press conferences can be waffly. You need more focus, and you need to be more collaborative.

Two years later, Albanese acknowledges winning that by-election was an "absolutely critical moment" for his leadership and for Labor during the last parliamentary term. "If we hadn't won that, the political dynamic would have been different," he says. But for the record, he doesn't like intervention as a description of the ensuing conversation with colleagues. He reframes: "There were constant assessments but no interventions."

Whether we label this an intervention or a constant assessment, several people point to this conversation, which has remained private until now, as an important milestone. Not a shoulder tap or an insurrection, or anything close. If anything, it was an expression of loyalty. But fealty rituals often expose the counterfactual. Bowen and Albanese get on well, but some believe Bowen's presence at the pep talk would have been unsettling, because if trouble were brewing for Albanese, it would come from elements of Bowen's Right faction. It wasn't clear from Albanese's reaction in the room how he had interpreted the feedback about his performance, but events afterwards suggest he listened.

Albanese went to work on both the front-facing elements of leadership and the elements that are invisible to voters. The front-end stuff was in part communicating more clearly, which is a journey of increments. Then there's the glow-up. Albanese losing weight and optimising his wardrobe is the least interesting thing that happened over his three years as Opposition leader, but it sent a critical message to the colleagues. It told them: I want to win enough to change the habits of a lifetime. Anyone of Irish-Italian heritage understands how hard it is to give up carbohydrates.

Towards the end of 2020 the Labor leader was in a lift with Michelle Rowland and a couple of other people at the Commonwealth Parliamentary Office in Sydney. Rowland – a communications lawyer before she entered politics – had embarked upon an extraordinary physical transformation a couple of years prior, shedding half her bodyweight through a keto diet and regular exercise. Rowland believed that not only had the weight loss been good for her physical health, it had improved her mental clarity as well. Albanese asked her how she'd managed to lose the kilograms. She told him there's no magic, you just have to be persistent. The answer was time, effort, willpower, consistency. The two resolved to have another, more detailed conversation about specifics, and from there a private dialogue started.

Rowland is horrified when I call her to ask what advice she supplied, because she had assured Albanese any conversation they ever had about weight loss would remain private. I put her mind at rest by telling her that as Albanese started to shed the weight, he was fond of telling colleagues he'd "been on the Michelle Rowland diet." That's how I had put two and two together. "This is not my news to break," Rowland says, still concerned this could look like fat-shaming. "I was prepared to share knowledge about what I had learnt, and I let him know I was there to support him and I wasn't going to tell anyone." She adds that Albanese didn't need a coach or an enforcer – he was incredibly disciplined about changing diet and lifestyle because he'd sought the change. The motivation had come from him.

There were also new glasses, which, in the way of things, generated a media frisson, including speculation about whether Labor had brought in an image consultant. Albanese was annoyed by the supposition he'd been Queer Eye'd, but some colleagues thought it was a hoot. They enjoyed imagining a world where gurus arrived and Albanese dutifully followed their instructions, because that would be a first, given he becomes even more doggedly mercurial when he suspects he's being managed. Albanese went to the local optometrist and picked the frames himself. Some colleagues were worried about what he might come back with, but the glasses were fine and there was an early measure of success. The glow-up gave Morrison the grumps. "Leopards don't change their spots, even if they change their glasses," he huffed. "I'm not pretending to be someone else."

What happened in the back rooms of Albanese's leadership project was far more significant. Albanese attempted to evolve from lone wolf to collaborative actor. That's a difficult transformation. The old dog for the hard road had to learn some new tricks. Albanese – who does not love process – learnt to create structures ensuring he maintained a stable bedrock of support. That meant tending relationships in both the NSW Right and Left factions, the national Left, parts of the Victorian Right and with key trade unions. To put this bluntly, Albanese had to learn to draw on a wider circle of advice and support than Wong and Butler, and if he was suspicious of the intentions of Shorten and his forces (for the record, he was), he needed to neutralise any threat. Good relationships with right-wingers Richard Marles and Don Farrell were critically important.

Insurgents always operate on a need-to-know basis, because widening the circle of trust creates existential risk. Establishment leaders need strategies of inclusivity. It is great to have two or three confidants who would take a bullet for you, but it's better to have ten or fifteen people. After so long in the trenches, after so many years having to push his way in and work three times as hard for every victory, Albanese needed to learn that leading the Labor Party wasn't a hostile takeover or a solo act. Most colleagues wanted him to succeed. Colleagues and subordinates needed opportunities to demonstrate their value. This was a completely different mindset.

As well as trusting the scaffolding, Albanese picked up some nuances in chairing meetings. He learnt leaders should never telegraph their own view too early, because that can shut down deliberation that often leads a group to a better landing point. Another skill was ensuring the deliberative processes operated as inclusively as possible, consistent with the standard political paranoia that sensitive things would leak. Part of inclusive management involved bringing colleagues in and allowing them to ventilate their issues. This happened iteratively during the first year of his leadership. After discovering during a couple of shadow cabinet processes that key colleagues couldn't read his mind, he learnt to consult senior leadership before nosing issues into that forum. The tweak allowed people to help him shape the final outcome in the room.

The pandemic also helped by necessitating regular internal dialogue. The Labor leadership group gathered almost weekly in conclave with the economic team and the shadow health minister. Over time, variations of that cohort became an expanded leadership group that engaged in broader deliberations, tossing around policy ideas and war-gaming what was coming up. In time, the leadership-plus group (Albanese, Marles, Wong, Kristina Keneally, Farrell, Katy Gallagher, Jim Chalmers, Tony Burke, Bowen and Butler) was dubbed the 4 p.m. group because that was the most regular time for phone hook-ups.

Albanese also met separately with Chalmers and Gallagher, the economic team. This weekly phone call began in the second half of 2021. Initially, that three-way conversation was about what was coming up in the Expenditure Review Committee of the shadow cabinet, but it evolved into a much broader forum for conversation. Then there was the Sunday night dinner group. On Sunday nights, ahead of parliamentary sitting weeks, Albanese would eat with Marles, Wong and Keneally, with semi-regular appearances from Bowen, Farrell, Burke, Chalmers and Gallagher. That ritual created more opportunities for people to be heard.

Caucusing in huddles like this was a significant change of modus operandi for Albanese. Once upon a time, he would have winged it, or crashed through impediments with guerrilla warfare. Colleagues say changing these habits, allowing people the opportunity to prove their worth to the operation, was one of the ways he grew in the job. The group also better understood some of what he needed to function optimally as leader: they should turn up to meetings on time, speak up in shadow cabinet, don't waste a deliberation, but if there was particularly difficult or sensitive feedback to be given, do it in private. Albanese does not like to be bounced in front of an audience. Few of us do.

Gallagher says when he became leader, "the tendency of the lone wolf approach was there because that's his natural way, but he's had to realise that once you step into that job as alternate prime minister you do need to rely on others and take others' advice, and go with your judgment 90 per cent of the time, but 10 per cent of the time it's good to have others either doing the job or advising you about the best way forward.

"I think he's done a good job with that because if you understand how his brain works, that tendency, the way he likes things done, I think that's a really hard adjustment – to rely on others and know you can't be the one who does everything, and as prime minister you shouldn't be the one who does everything."

Chalmers says the growth went two ways. It was in Albanese's interests to reach out, but colleagues also had to rise to the occasion. "The onus was on the rest of us to prove our worth to him and the team and to earn his trust," the treasurer says. Chalmers thinks the first time voters would have clocked the collegiate tendency was during the election campaign, when a bout of Covid took Albanese off the hustings for a week and shadow ministers had to fill the void. The required transition in the campaign looked seamless from the outside because by then, the group was used to operating as a collective. By the time voters noticed the comparative lack of presidential trappings and tone in the Labor campaign, the team inclination had become hardwired in both Albanese and the operation. In contrast to the two-person government of Morrison and Frydenberg, a contrast that became useful politically as well as substantively, Chalmers says Albanese put the team as "a feature of his leadership."

A couple of quick vignettes. A few weeks after the election, a friend of mine, an experienced Canberra public servant, expressed relief and some surprise that Cabinet government was back. According to this account, the bureaucracy had become very used to the Morrison/Frydenberg show. People had forgotten ministers spoke up in meetings and sought to drive their own agendas. Another vignette comes from the Lodge. Shortly after the victory, Albanese had his colleagues over to the Canberra residence. People say the prime minister became emotional about how the team had rallied over the three years of Opposition, and particularly during the campaign. If you wonder why something as mundane as teamwork can be a point of emotion, think about the Rudd–Gillard civil war. I doubt it was only Albanese shedding a quiet tear of relief. I suspect some other veterans may have as well, while touching wood in the hope that the esprit de corps could survive the pressures and complexities of government.

I'm curious about whether Albanese is self-aware about the skills he had to acquire to lead a group. Does he think he went into the job knowing how to be the Labor leader?

"No," he says. "You don't always get it right."

Are you still learning?

"Of course," he says. "I learn stuff every day." This response is true enough, but I'd like a deeper dive. But Albanese is already up in his helicopter surveying his accumulated life experiences. "You learn from how you do things, you learn policy stuff … I think I learnt a lot at international forums that I've done, you learn about different cultures and building relationships. You pick up the skills that you pick up in the Labor Party over a long period of time. You learn from that."

"Action, reaction, action, reaction. Are we where we need to be? All the interactions you have — you learn and grow as a person."

HONING A CALL TO ACTION: CHILDCARE AND CLIMATE CHANGE

Mastering machine politics, acquiring power, learning to lead – what is it all for? Why spend a lifetime accumulating these tools? Ambitious politicians want to change the country, so walk with me down the policy formulation road. We've established that Albanese finessing the external and internal arts of party leadership was critically important to convincing his colleagues and Australians he was ready for the prime ministership. But he wouldn't just be selling himself at the 2022 election. Labor's policy offering also had to be resolved. The resolution of the election platform gives us useful insight into how Albanese deliberates and decides. We'll consider two case studies. The first is childcare, the second climate change, which will be a key issue over this parliamentary term.

By October 2020, Albanese had made a captain's call. He was going to spend $6 billion on childcare, and that policy was going to be the centrepiece of his budget reply speech. This decision was chewed over for weeks in the leadership group and the shadow Expenditure Review Committee, and it continued to be contested vigorously right up until a couple of hours before it was unveiled. The fiscal implications were the primary concern for Albanese's colleagues. Did enough people care about childcare to deliver a political dividend commensurate with the investment? And what would allocating dollars there mean for spending on other pressing needs, like aged care?

Albanese was strongly in favour of proceeding, but gesturing to the collective equivocation, he opened the door to fretful colleagues. He told them, I think this is the right way to go, but if you've got a better idea, bring it to me. Ideas percolated up, but they weren't better ideas, which was the leader's benchmark. In the absence of a compelling alternative, childcare went to the full shadow cabinet late on the day it was announced. Some say the only steadfast supporters of the policy Albanese outlined on the evening of 8 October, apart from the leader, were the architect of the policy initiative, Amanda Rishworth, then shadow minister for early childhood education, and one of her key supporters, Don Farrell, the South Australian right-wing powerbroker.

"Childcare was 100 per cent him," Katy Gallagher says, meaning Albanese. "Amanda had done the policy work obviously, but it was one of his first announcements, it set the scene for the election contest really, and it created a fiscal gap in the order of five and a half billion dollars, so that decision really meant we were never going to have a better bottom line than the government."

Albanese acknowledges the decision was contested internally, but says he was clear in his own mind that childcare needed to be a priority. Childcare was a vital service. It wasn't complicated. Investment there would build a political bridge to Australia's harried working mothers – a cohort Morrison didn't seem particularly interested in speaking to – and it would also give Labor a modern productivity story, because good childcare encourages women into paid work, and higher labour market participation drives economic growth. A productivity story was also a bridge to the business community.

Georgie Dent, executive director of The Parenthood, recounts the political atmospherics surrounding the decision. "That week, Morrison and Frydenberg had handed down a budget that quite sensationally overlooked women despite the well documented burden they were carrying throughout Covid," she says. Dent had made that point sharply in the public domain and her critique gained some traction. Morrison's office was irritated by the backchat. "The phone call I received from a PMO staffer telling me that their budget wasn't gendered, and that no one credible was criticising their budget, led to a #CredibleWomen hashtag going viral," she says.

Dent says Morrison's dismissive response at that time was the beginning of a backlash that became highly problematic for Morrison – the mobilisation of professional women against the government. She believes Labor's childcare policy was a turning point for Albanese. "Aside from being compelling policy, childcare was politically astute, and it was also courageous given the ALP's fear from May 2019 that a bold early learning commitment was politically dangerous," she says. "That childcare commitment was the first step towards winning office."

While acknowledging the decision was a hard-edged political assessment, Albanese was attracted to the policy by something more essential to his inclinations as a life-taught progressive. It was the idea of childcare becoming a universal service, like Medicare or superannuation. Labor's election policy didn't extend as far as universality, but Albanese made it clear that was where Labor was going with childcare reform. Albanese was attracted to childcare as a new social compact. Meredith Burgmann says Albanese is a product of "classic 1970s, 1980s leftism – that's the tradition he comes out of." What she means is that he is comfortable with social engineering. She says that's why he's grabbed the Voice to Parliament so early in his prime ministership; it's the same motivation. Using the power of government to level up.

Albanese believes childcare can change the trajectory for kids from disadvantaged backgrounds. He was a "voracious reader" when he was a kid. "Mum drummed that into me. Most kids from working-class backgrounds don't have that and that was a huge advantage I had. I read history books. That put me in good stead." He says his end goal of universality for childcare in Australia gives all kids, regardless of their background, access to early learning, and that can make a material difference in a person's life because some kids don't have engaged or aspirational parents. "It's good bloody policy," he says. "All kids need access to those opportunities, and the shift towards universality, I've made it very clear that's where I'm headed."

Albanese says making that decision was hard for colleagues because of the cognitive dissonance. "We had just been defeated in an election because people said we had too much radical policy and I was going to the first budget reply with a radical new policy that was costing a lot of money, including lifting the payments to people earning up to $530,000 a year, and saying that's a first step to doing it across the board."

Gallagher says the shadow cabinet was "on the childcare wagon, but we had different views about cut-offs and those sorts of things and creating a big fiscal problem when we didn't know that state of things." In the middle of the clutter, neck deep in the complications of a complicated system, Albanese pulled his head above it, and focused on the strategic call. "He's not a token when it comes to women's rights," Gallagher says. "He got it before the common understanding of economic participation of women, the inhibitors, what they might be, and affordability.

"He spoke about all that before the reports started coming out that supported our position and he was adamant and clear. There are moments when leaders just have to make a call because they don't get a single opinion. That's a real test of leadership, I reckon. He made the call and we all bunked in."

That 2020 budget reply also contained the first instalment of the most difficult internal and external undertaking of the term: settling Labor's climate policy. Alongside childcare, Albanese unveiled a plan for a $20-billion corporation to build electricity transmission infrastructure to prepare Australia's power grid for renewables. While there could be agreement around this measure, everything else was still up for grabs, including where Labor would land in setting a new emissions reduction target for 2030. Resolving the target was generating significant heat.

The veteran NSW right-winger Joel Fitzgibbon had faced a massive swing against him in 2019 in his coal seat in the Hunter Valley. The near-death experience put the fear of God into him. He began a campaign for Labor to adopt the same 2030 target as the government. The then shadow climate change minister, Mark Butler, was implacably opposed to the capitulation on ambition that Fitzgibbon was proselytising. Butler dug in, and the two sparred in public.

From the outside, this conflict looked impossible to resolve. Fitzgibbon was an old mate of Albanese's from the parliamentary class of 1996, and Butler was one of the leader's closest personal friends and factional allies. Fitzgibbon escalated, advocating for Butler's removal from the portfolio.

Again, from the outside, finding a resolution looked impossible. Albanese was very unlikely to move Butler if he wanted to remain in the portfolio and Butler was giving no signals publicly about retreating.

But behind the scenes, Albanese's inner circle contemplated shifting the shadow ministerial deckchairs to try to neutralise the brawling. Wong is Labor's Ms Fixit. Before Albanese broadened his structures for advice, Wong was deputised periodically as the colleague with sufficient cut-through to carry a difficult message to the leader.

In the middle of 2020, Wong was counselling Albanese to execute a portfolio swap between Butler and Chris Bowen. Butler and Bowen have a good personal relationship, and they agreed on the need to maintain as much policy ambition as possible. Bowen, like Fitzgibbon, is from the NSW Right, but the two right-wingers were at odds when it came to climate action.

Butler had asked Bowen during a particularly grim phase of his battle with Fitzgibbon whether it would be better for everyone if climate change had a different figurehead. The realpolitik was simple: if the climate portfolio was held by a senior figure from the Right faction, it would be much harder for Right-faction mischief makers to go to war with Bowen.

At the time, Bowen rebuffed Butler's overture. But he reconsidered in the months that followed, attracted to the idea of framing climate action as the unfinished element of the economic reforms Labor had pursued since the early 1980s. Bowen revisited the swap idea with Butler, who then put the idea to Albanese. Wong was supportive. Albanese then called Bowen to make sure he was on board.

Butler believes it was important that he remained in the climate portfolio immediately after the election defeat in 2019 to demonstrate that Labor would recalibrate the policy but not shift on the fundamentals. But he thinks his presence after that point became counterproductive.

"Anthony was committed to finding a way to having a strong climate policy and reconnecting with the people in the Hunter and central Queensland that we, slash I, repelled in 2019, and I think he did that," he says. "Me moving was essential to that. I'd become not a totem but a symbol, and me staying there was being presented as a sign that we could never do anything other than what we'd done in 2019, we couldn't nuance [the policy], we weren't up for discussion about it."

Albanese says Fitzgibbon's theatrics made it harder to execute the personnel shift they all felt was needed to land the policy they wanted to land. He says Butler wanted Health, Bowen wanted Climate and would pitch the transition using the language of a former treasurer, which everyone hoped would reset the debate. "But [Butler] moving became more difficult because people were calling for it," Albanese says. "That wasn't helpful."

By November, Fitzgibbon was off the front bench after a blazing row in shadow cabinet about whether or not he was a team player. Albanese had begun the meeting criticising ill-disciplined commentary. Joe Biden had just beaten Donald Trump. Labor's plan had been to use the defeat of Trump to restate the case for ambitious climate action now that Biden would return the United States to the Paris Agreement. Biden's victory also put Morrison on the move. Understanding there would be pressure from the new administration, the prime minister floated Australia moving to net zero emissions by 2050. Fitzgibbon cut across Labor's planned media blitz with a deliberate strike, describing colleagues as "delusional" for taking comfort from the Biden victory. Given only one person in the room met the criteria for ill-discipline, but Albanese hadn't named him, Fitzgibbon retorted: "I'm in the room, you shouldn't speak about me like I'm not here." A rhetorical melee ensued.

At this juncture, it looked like the climate policy redux was in significant danger of being crunched in a proxy war between the Right and Left factions that could easily escalate to leadership conflagration. There was rampant leaking, and peacocking, and by this point Canberra had entered the annual killing season.

Media speculation about whether Albanese would go the distance was rife and it grew over the summer. The whole operation looked unstable. Albanese ignored the static and the Bowen/Butler swap was locked in by December 2020, but this plan remained undisclosed to the voters and many of the colleagues. It remained under wraps until the news leaked just ahead of the shadow ministerial reshuffle Albanese unveiled at the start of 2021.

In between the personnel swap being locked in and the full reshuffle Albanese unveiled on 28 January, the Labor leader came face to face with his own mortality. As he told me several months later, for a few seconds between braking and the crunch of metal, "I thought, this is how it ends."

Deus ex machina

Albanese finished up tasks in his electorate office late on Friday, 8 January 2021. He got into his Toyota and began the drive home. When he reached Hill Street in Marrickville, a Range Rover ploughed head-on into the driver's side of his car. At the point of impact, Albanese feared he would die. He ended up in hospital with serious injuries. Full recovery took time and protracted medical attention — more than he confessed to at the time.

The accident has assumed semi-mythical status in the history of Albanese's journey to the prime ministership; an instance of deus ex machina: after the car crash, everything changed. You do hear this version of events semi-regularly. Did *everything* change, though?

Albanese was certainly shaken afterwards, and unsteady as he recovered, plagued by dizziness and other physical aftershocks. I remember one of the early post-crash press conferences where he sucked down what looked like a litre of water and gripped the podium to steady himself. Rather than being possessed by a new, Zen-like clarity that prompted a fundamental life change, Albanese got angry. You could see it. He was ropable that some colleagues continued to brief that he wasn't up to the task of beating Morrison while he was recovering from a crash that could have killed him. You could see the frustration gathering like a minor Pacific typhoon. His dander was well and truly up.

Albanese had already resolved to execute a scrub-up and sharpen-up strategy. That was in train. Albanese is a confidence player, but like all intelligent and self-aware people, he doubts. *Can I do this?* The shock of the accident did seem to resolve, once and for all, that he was not going to be Labor's nightwatchman. He was going to come for Morrison, and for anyone who stood between him and that objective, including disloyal colleagues. I could see his frustration: *Screw all of you. You think I can't beat this bloke? Strap in. Watch me.*

The prime minister recounts his state of mind more neutrally, although the moral of the story is clear. "The only time during the term ... [Albanese pauses and recalibrates slightly] ... I was never very worried about Joel or the internal rumbling, the only time I went ouch was when I was in hospital and people were ringing journos and undermining me when I was injured. That was upsetting, to say the least, but I was determined to do the right thing, and I think it worked."

I'm interested in whether he thinks the accident was a turning point, per the lore.

"I was forward-leaning from that time," Albanese says. He says he went from "chilled" to playing political offence. Before the accident "I was determined to hold my nerve, people were looking for us to do more, come out with new policies, suggesting we do a climate policy in 2020. They were wrong. Including people who were close to me."

Albanese says he stuck rigidly to his own policy timetable but went on the front foot about personnel, risking some internal friction. There were basic problems that needed fixing, starting with the fact that all his leadership team were in security portfolios. Labor needed to train its sights on the economy and jobs and stitch climate action into that materialist narrative in the remaining time before the election. The process of delegitimising Morrison also needed to gather pace, and that project seemed more possible in the second year of the pandemic than it had in the first.

Marles was tweezered out of Defence and given Skills. Albanese effected the Bowen/Butler swap, and put the Victorian right-winger Clare O'Neil into Aged Care. "I thought that was really important," he says. A certain amount of ululating ensued from process obsessives like me about winners and losers in the reshuffle. We all read the tea leaves and stroked our chins on panel shows. "All of this got written up badly as if it was about personnel – none of it was about personnel, or rewarding or not rewarding people," Albanese says. "It was about what was needed."

With the reshuffle settled and the internal climate policy fight neutralised by Bowen's arrival in the portfolio and Fitzgibbon's departure from shadow cabinet, the Labor team ploughed into 2021. If 2020 was Morrison's best year in the top job, 2021 was his worst. He flailed on the supply of vaccines. He brawled with the premiers. He comprehensively botched federal parliament's #MeToo moment. The unravelling was a gift to Albanese, and Labor kept piling on the pressure. All that spectacle gave Labor plenty of cover to execute the most important decision of that year: where they would ultimately land on climate policy.

Before moving to Health, Butler had resolved that external analysts would undertake an economic assessment of the new climate policy to ensure Labor was not marooned as it had been during the 2019 election, unable to answer specific questions about the costs and consequence of its emissions reduction targets and policy mechanisms to drive the transition to low emissions. Labor engaged RepuTex – specialists in this field. "We spent a lot of money doing that," Albanese says.

But it wasn't just the *what* of the policy animating the brains trust. Albanese also thought the timing of the announcement would be critical. Almost every time Albanese fronted the media, he got the same question: what would the 2030 target be? "We were asked this every day for two years," Albanese says. "We didn't succumb to pressure." Labor was conscious Morrison was battling his own internal divisions as he attempted to land a Coalition commitment to achieving net zero emissions by 2050. Morrison would have to declare a position at the United Nations climate talks in Glasgow in November 2021. Albanese felt it would be best for Labor to unveil its climate policy "after Glasgow, after [Morrison's] non-position." He was looking for a political sweet spot – after Glasgow, but not so close to an election that Labor could be accused of hiding something dastardly.

Albanese's calculation was that if he could find the sweet spot, Morrison would have significant difficulty responding because he was wedged between two constituencies – centre-right progressives in the cities sick to death of the Coalition weaponising climate action, and the voters in the regions that the Coalition had radicalised against climate action during the 2013 and 2019 contests.

Butler thinks two developments were critical in bolstering Labor's case for sticking with a higher medium-term target than the Coalition: the defeat of Donald Trump in the US presidential election in late 2020, and the Business Council of Australia's volte-face domestically. During the 2019 election, the BCA had characterised Labor's 45 per cent emissions reduction target as "economy-wrecking." But business in Australia had shifted. Butler says sentiment moved here in part because Australia had passed the peak of the mining boom, but he thinks the real turning point was the taskforce on climate-related disclosure – "the way that percolated through the international financial system in a year or eighteen months."

The taskforce Butler is referring to is a creature of the Financial Stability Board, an international body that makes recommendations about regulatory shifts in the global financial system to support investors, banks and financial institutions and their underwriters to identify and price risks related to climate change. "That completely transformed things, Black Rock, insurance investors, banks, everyone suddenly went, ah okay, [carbon risk] is real, directors will be legally and financially liable for these decisions," he says. Bowen thinks the shift in the Liberal Party, particularly in New South Wales, where the state climate minister Matt Kean was out making a case for ambitious action, also helped.

Bowen came to the policy deliberation with fresh eyes. This was very important, because Labor's veterans of the climate wars were weary after having lost every round of the argument since 2013. By the time he arrived in the portfolio, the BCA was also signalling to the Opposition directly that it intended to support higher emissions reduction targets.

Through 2021, Labor considered two potential landing points. The first was a defensive play – unveil a 2030 emissions target in the low to mid-thirties, accompanied by support for renewables and transition grants for industrial polluters – the sector of the economy known as emissions-intensive, trade-exposed businesses. Mines. Gas producers. Smelters. The second involved continuing to prosecute a case for ambition. This meant a 2030 target somewhere in the forties or perhaps early fifties and engaging the Abbott-era safeguard mechanism to drive down industrial pollution. A number of people say Bowen favoured ambition at the upper end of that range. He was all in.

A quick word of explanation about the safeguard mechanism. When the Coalition repealed Labor's carbon price, the Abbott government established the safeguard ostensibly to keep pollution from big emitters in check. The mechanism never worked per the stated intention, because it was designed to fail. But Labor's view (and the view of business) was that the safeguard framework could be made to work. The scheme would need a new 2030 emissions reduction target, and clear rules to ensure net emissions were kept below a specified limit or "baseline."

Albanese was not keen on the target being 45 per cent, given the torrid history in the 2019 campaign. He was also firmly against the defensive play as the preferred option and communicated that to people on several occasions. Albanese told the portfolio ministers that in the event he lost the 2022 election, he did not want to look back and conclude that he'd failed to prosecute an evidence-based argument on climate change. But doubts persisted in the leadership group. A number of people were worried that a higher target meant political slaughter. Bowen wasn't interested in tokenism, and dug in.

When the drafts of the RepuTex work eventually landed, shadow ministers and staff met daily to go through the material with a fine-tooth comb, looking for wrinkles the government or hostile stakeholders could weaponise. At one point, the pencilled-in number for the 2030 target was 42 per cent, which would have tickled devotees of *The Hitchhiker's Guide to the Galaxy* – 42 being the answer to the ultimate question of life, the universe and everything. Albanese says the final number, 43 per cent, was decided in the week Labor announced its climate policy.

The leadership group was in the loop about the direction of the policy-making. The Sunday night dinner group also met two or three times in the week before the policy was unveiled. There wasn't unanimity. People were nervous. Some say the internal pushback over that final week was full throated – significant enough to derail Bowen's policy. Like childcare, the climate package did not go to the full shadow cabinet until the day it was set to be unveiled. Albanese was always concerned about leaks, and justifiably so, because sensitive things did leak periodically with an objective of causing harm. Labor's decision to back the Morrison government's commitment to the AUKUS submarine pact was another critical call that was assessed by shadow cabinet in almost real time – that is, just before the decision was announced.

Albanese knew business endorsement of the climate policy would be critical for Labor politically. In November, he had dinner with Jennifer Westacott, then chief executive of the BCA, and its president, Tim Reed. A number of Labor figures see Reed as the driving intellectual force behind the shift in the business lobby, a shift that reflected the BCA's changing membership. Also interesting in this regard: Albanese is close to Mike Cannon-Brookes, the billionaire co-founder of the tech firm Atlassian. Cannon-Brookes has been banging the drum publicly for a couple of years about the need to address the climate crisis. Albanese has also known Westacott for twenty years, since she was a state bureaucrat in New South Wales and Victoria. "I said, here's where I think we are going ... we talked it through," Albanese says. "I didn't give them specifics because we hadn't landed yet."

He left the catch-up reasonably confident the BCA would endorse the policy, at least in principle, "so if you had the BCA and the ACTU, then there's a fair chance you are on the road to getting a discussion." Labor was also consulting with the Ai Group – which had led the business community advocating for a reboot of the safeguard mechanism to drive emissions reduction – the Australian Chamber of Commerce and Industry, the National Farmers' Federation and the Australian Conservation Foundation.

On 3 December the whole package – the targets and safeguard mechanism adjustments – went to the Expenditure Review Committee of shadow cabinet, then the shadow cabinet, and then the caucus. While the key stakeholders had been lined up, the nervousness in the Sunday night dinner group spilled over into a collective anxiety attack in the shadow cabinet. Even people who had been absolutely steadfast through previous policy rounds of the climate wars panicked at the final hurdle. How would 43 per cent play in outer-suburban marginals? The question that no one could answer with any certainty hung heavily in the air: are we just signing away winning the next election? Again? How many times are we going to do this?

Everyone knew the climate decision was the biggest roll of the dice in Albanese's time as Labor leader. During the pandemic, Albanese had pursued a strategy of soft opposition. The overarching objective was to delegitimise Morrison, weaponise his mistakes against him, but not to ambulance-chase on policy. Agree to as much of the Coalition's policy agenda as possible, including the unaffordable stage three tax cuts, to reduce the size of the battlefield.

Most of the conflict of the term was around personality and process. Albanese chose clear product differentiation on two substantive things that were important for him and for Labor definitionally. The first was childcare, for the reasons we've already canvassed. The second was climate change. Opinion polls through the term showed a significant cohort of voters struggled to get a fix on him. He needed policy ballast to define his leadership and to give equivocal voters a concrete call to action. Everybody sitting around the shadow cabinet table knew a climate fight in the 2022 contest would be material to the outcome. What was then unknown was whether Labor would be sailing into more lethal headwinds, or whether the wind would finally be at their back.

Because of the internal angst, Bowen came to shadow cabinet heavily prepared. He gave a presentation to demonstrate his ability to communicate the policy to voters in cut-through language. When colleagues wondered how the 43 per cent target would play in western Sydney and regional Queensland, Bowen told colleagues Labor would be arguing for 600,000 new jobs, an electricity grid powered with 82 per cent renewable energy, and $72 billion worth of new investment. Bowen's shadow assistant minister Pat Conroy, in the outer shadow ministry but drafted for the occasion, said Labor would be able to be very clear with voters in regional seats who were fearful about the transition. The RepuTex Energy modelling made it clear that not a single coalfired power station would close early. He said energy-intensive trade-exposed industries would also not face more onerous regulations here than their competitors faced overseas.

Albanese says getting to this point was "difficult, both internally and externally." He wanted to ensure the policy was as bulletproof as possible. No respectable stakeholders out decrying the measures as economy-wrecking. "We had to get that moment," he says. Back in 2019, achieving that moment had seemed absolutely impossible. Albanese also points to it as evidence of his professional growth as Labor leader. In his youth, he would have gone to war with the naysayers. These days, his objective is to navigate through to consensus.

Bowen believes the climate policy Labor took to the 2022 election was critical, not only substantively for the country, but electorally. "We wouldn't have won Higgins, Bennelong, Reid without a decent climate policy," he says. "We got positive swings in central Queensland and held our territory." He says having a more ambitious policy offering than the Coalition gave impetus to the teal independents and their campaigns because centre-right progressive voters could see there was value in a change of government, even if they couldn't bring themselves to vote Labor. "If we had just matched the government on climate targets, we wouldn't have won those seats and probably those voters in Wentworth and Kooyong would have said, what's the point? We can't change anything, so what's the point?"

The point of recounting all this history is simple. We can't fathom the future without understanding the past. We can't know how Albanese will approach the prime ministership if we don't understand how he got there, his motivations and how he operates. When we pull all these threads together, this is what we can deduce about Australia's thirty-first prime minister.

Albanese is a lifelong progressive, with a sharp class consciousness, but he's not a policy purist – he'll always take something over nothing.

Like his mentor Tom Uren, his political values are drawn from life, not philosophy or theory.

He's a working-class scrapper with the smarts and the persistence to enter the elites. He could have been Mark Latham. Their backgrounds are very similar. But he's chosen to be Anthony Albanese rather than burning through Labor, teaming up with Pauline Hanson and railing against wokeness on Sky News.

He is aspirational, because he's self-made, and he's self-centred, but not narcissistic.

Having been underestimated most of his life, he's learnt that ambiguity can be a superpower as valuable as authority. It's easier to change the world, bit by bit, to change power balances in society, if no one sees you coming.

He's a clever and patient strategist, with sharp political judgment. Power is his natural habitat, and he's spent a lifetime studying all its forms, covert and overt. In order of preference, Albanese is fascinated by power, politics, parliament, policy and process.

He sets store on being a good person. Friend is a word with meaning. He's all the life-affirming human things – joyful, droll, doggedly loyal, kind, instinctual, emotional and impatient; and he's all the political things – hyper-rational, calculating, exclusionary and retributive if you mean to thwart him.

He likes control, of his time, of his environment. He needs a crowd, because a diverse and well-maintained network always gives a person options, but he also needs to be alone, in his head, running scenarios.

He's learning to think in a group setting after a professional lifetime of strategising alone. He understands colleagues need to do their thing. But he doesn't like to be pinned down, or corralled, or managed. He can still lose his temper, although he's trying to do that less often. It can be hard to know what's going on inside his head.

Albanese plays a long game. He understands the best way to achieve progress is to stay alive, and to cut your cloth to suit the times.

Given Wong's closeness to Albanese, and her centrality in many of these processes, I ask her to nominate the most important decision he made over the three years in Opposition. Wong says Anthony decided not to die wondering.

"He decided he wanted to win, I guess that's the most important decision," Wong says. "He decided he was not going to lose. If you are asking what is the psychological decision as opposed to political decisions, he decided to win, and he wanted to win the prime ministership, not the leadership of the Labor Party."

Albanese puts his assessment of the path to victory slightly differently. Plague year 2020 "was what it was." You had to know when to dive under the dumper and when to get out your boogie board and start paddling to catch the wave as it crested. "I held my nerve," Albanese says. "More than anyone else. I held my nerve."

While Albanese ploughed into his metaphorical ocean and waited for the right time to surface, other political actors were scouting on jetskis as the sets rolled in. Simon Holmes à Court is in Rome when we speak. I can hear the ambulances careening around in the background, those distinctive sirens. The founder of Climate 200 is explaining the difference between what happened in the election in 2019 and what happened in 2022.

"We caught a wave," he says, cheerily. "The zeitgeist was different. There was a huge wave this time. Instead of sitting on the shore watching the wave, we had built a really good surfboard and we were in the water paddling. We were ready when it came and we rode it all the way to the shore."

Caught it is something of an understatement. We know what happened on 21 May. Voters turned their backs on Scott Morrison. Australians elected a progressive parliament. Between Labor, teal and Green gains around the country, the electoral repudiation of the Coalition was comprehensive enough to feel visceral. The Liberal Party lost seventeen seats. Labor got to seventy-seven seats and majority government. The Greens gained ground in the lower house and are the major balance-of-power players in the Senate. A new progressive independent senator for the Australian Capital Territory, David Pocock, is the Brian Harradine of this parliament, occupying a kingmaking spot.

If you follow politics, you'll know the major-party vote has been declining in Australia for years. According to research by the Parliamentary Library, over the four decades from the 1950s to the 1980s the major parties received more than 90 per cent of the total first-preference votes in House of Representatives elections, on average. By 1998, that figure was down to 79.6 per cent. In the 2010s, Australian Electoral Commission figures show it averaged 78 per cent. On 21 May 2022, it dropped to just over 68 per cent. The Coalition's primary vote fell nearly six points to 35.7 per cent and the Labor primary vote was 32.6 per cent, down almost one point.

Australian National University academics Nicholas Biddle and Ian McAllister noted in a paper published shortly after the election that 68.3 per cent of voters giving their first preference to the major parties was a historic low, and suggested the 2022 election "may have ushered in a major realignment in Australian voting, with the election of six teal independents in previously staunch Liberal party seats, a dramatic increase in the number of Greens MPs concentrated in Brisbane, and the lowest primary vote ever for an incoming government." Australians didn't only rinse the three-term Coalition incumbents; in the major cities and some regional areas, they voted for a different kind of representation. A new kind of politics: local, values-based, aspirational.

It is worth unpacking the campaign dynamics and we can do that by speaking to some of the actors disrupting the status quo. Holmes à Court is an energy analyst and investor, and son of the late Robert Holmes à Court, the billionaire corporate raider and philanthropist, and his formidable wife, Janet. He set up Climate 200 in 2019 out of frustration. All the great ideas associated with the transition to low emissions were hitting a brick wall in Canberra. Watching the wretched climate wars from the sidelines, Holmes à Court formed the view Australia needed a majority of MPs with a science-based approach to climate change. Politics needed a dose of integrity. The events of 2021 also added a third value: advancing the treatment of and respect for women in Australia, whether it's in the community, the workplace or politics.

Holmes à Court doesn't characterise the phenomenon this way, and he may not love the comparison, but if we consider the problem through the Holmes à Court family lens, Australian politics was behaving like a distressed asset, and Climate 200 was part of supercharging a takeover strategy that had been underway for several years with the "Voices of" independents movement. There is a long history of independents in Australian parliaments. Two men – Tony Windsor and Rob Oakeshott – were kingmakers in the forty-third parliament, where Julia Gillard governed in minority. But it was the Victorian Cathy McGowan who pioneered a people-powered model of community organising called Voices for Indi, which was the engine room of her successful election to a federal seat in 2013. McGowan's group conducted fifty-three "kitchen-table" conversations in the seat of Indi in the run-up to the 2013 election. Rather than imposing a set of policies on constituents, the voters drove the agenda. McGowan modelled how to do politics differently, and made sure the model she pioneered was replicable in electorates around the country.

Holmes à Court first entered the fray in the 2019 election, making financial contributions to climate-focused independents. It was a dry run and he wasn't experienced. Climate 200 was established six weeks before the 2019 contest, but most of the donations came in the closing fortnight. There were thirty donors and the group raised about half a million dollars.

By the time the 2022 contest rolled around, the group was operating at a whole other level of professionalism. Holmes à Court engaged Anthony Reed, a former Labor strategist who had spearheaded the Wentworth by-election campaign in 2018 that propelled Kerryn Phelps into federal parliament, and the 2019 campaign that saw Zali Steggall defeat Tony Abbott in Warringah. He met Byron Fay when Fay was working for the South Australian Senate independent Tim Storer. "I engaged both of them about a year and a half out," Holmes à Court says. "I said, in six weeks we did this, what would you do if we had a full year? They wrote me a review on what I did right and what I did wrong and what to do differently if I wanted to have a bigger effect."

Separate to this, the "Voices of" structure was chugging along under its own steam, preparing for the 2022 contest. McGowan says Holmes à Court started pulling together money from a network of environmental benefactors in Australia. "He was looking at seats that could be swung," she says. "So, he's bubbling along minding his own business, and I'm aware of what he is doing because people on the ground are coming to me and asking what I know about what's going on." McGowan says the first time she met Holmes à Court was in Melbourne in October 2020. This conversation traversed their commonalities and differences. "Very early in the piece, we had a discussion about our approach," McGowan says. "We were grassroots, we were not fundraising and we were building community from the bottom up. I just let him know we knew stuff, but also that his stuff is different."

They continued on in their respective lanes. By February 2021, McGowan convened a community independents' convention by Zoom, with 300 people and 78-plus electorates represented. Holmes à Court dialled in with a couple of advisers.

"Afterwards, we talked about what we called swapping notes," McGowan says. "From here on in we operated – I wouldn't even say in parallel. If you can imagine two circles in a Venn diagram, they were their own circle doing fundraising and that sort of stuff, and we were our own circle doing community engagement work, building networks. And there was an overlap in the middle which we called swapping notes. From 2021 until 2022, we spoke monthly so we weren't treading on each other's toes."

Holmes à Court invited McGowan onto the advisory board of Climate 200. Several former politicians had joined. McGowan declined. "It was really important that we were independent of the money," she says. "We needed to be our own people. If they were giving out money, that was their business; it had nothing to do with anything I was doing." From McGowan's perspective, Climate 200 had cash and valuable campaign skills but their interventions were entirely strategic. They were focused on targeted interventions in winnable seats. She was a long-term community activist, and her "Voices of" model was about building community networks to force better representation regardless of the prospects of immediate electoral success. "Our [half of the] Venn diagram was much bigger than theirs," she says.

Armed with a concrete strategy, Holmes à Court scaled up his operation. "We raised a lot more money and brought on a lot of talent," he says. In 2019, Climate 200's interventions were below the radar. In 2022, the group picked up the loudhailer, "which not everybody in the community independents' movement loved." Not everyone in the media loved it either.

Self-evidently the group was raising money and wielding influence, and in a democracy that activity requires proper scrutiny and accountability, particularly given Australia's electoral disclosure regime has more holes in it than Swiss cheese. But the Murdoch press and the Fox News wannabes on the Sky News after-dark shift saw progressive conspiracy and went ballistic, unleashing a barrage of toxic coverage.

Ironically, all the ranting was helpful for name recognition. Often the biggest structural challenge independents face is telling voters who they are. News Corp became a free media machine for the teal campaigns. But while there was upside, a number of community independents did not love the attention Climate 200 was drawing to their contests. Tipping out major-party incumbents felt hard enough without all the static crackling around Holmes à Court and his operation. At the candidate and campaign level, there was a lot of trepidation about being taken out by friendly fire.

Holmes à Court kept pushing forward. He believed research would be a necessary precondition for success. Enter Kos Samaras, a long-time Labor operative who was now running strategy and campaigns for the Melbourne-based lobbying firm RedBridge. In December 2020, Voices of Kooyong, which was a campaign structure set up to assist Oliver Yates – an independent who took on Josh Frydenberg in 2019 – contacted Samaras and asked for some professional advice. In January, Samaras joined the group on Zoom – he recalls about sixty very enthusiastic people. Holmes à Court was in the audience. A day or two later Samaras got a call from Holmes à Court following up. He wanted to know whether it was possible for independents to take heartland seats from Liberal incumbents. "I said, look, demographically, the way these seats are changing, the types of people who live in them, yes, absolutely," Samaras says. "You just need to commit to it." Holmes à Court asked him to write up a proposal canvassing both the why and the how.

Samaras obliged. The why was demographic change. "Particular parts of these electorates are now problematic for the Coalition because they have high numbers of young professional women in particular and a renter cohort that is growing rapidly," Samaras says. "I went through a whole series of triggers." On this analysis, several Liberal heartland seats had "big red flags" – big enough to make them winnable. "We found out through research these people wanted to see significant change in the country, but they didn't like brand Labor and they thought the Greens were a bit extreme," Samaras says. "The Greens in Kooyong was not really going to work because there's not enough pragmatism about them."

The how was cash, candidates and competency. "All we needed to do was build a particular brand of politics that was going to fit nicely, and meet these needs that people had, that [was] sort of centrist, socially progressive, on climate very progressive, with a bit of pragmatism and a few other things," Samaras says.

The 2019 election had already delivered a proof of concept. Zali Steggall was in the parliament, having vanquished Tony Abbott on a climate action platform. So was Helen Haines, the independent member for Indi, who had held the Victorian regional seat after the departure of McGowan. Once in parliament, Steggall had pursued climate action through a private member's bill that garnered national attention. Haines had pursed a federal integrity commission so doggedly that the Liberal moderate Bridget Archer crossed the floor in an effort to bring on debate.

Steggall and Haines were sensible, articulate women who got things done. In the noxious atmospherics of 2021, when women and their allies were out in the streets marching for justice, a feminised political movement felt like a powerful scalable, salient prototype. Holmes à Court borrows a concept from his friend, the Atlassian founder and fellow climate activist Mike Cannon-Brookes. "Mike has this thing he calls lighthouse projects," he says. The simplest translation of a lighthouse project is something impossible becoming a thing, and by opening minds enabling a raft of new projects.

"I think Australians have a real problem with imagining things that don't exist," Holmes à Court says. "The big battery in South Australia was a lighthouse project. A Northern Territory solar farm that feeds Singapore is impossible, but once it happens we'll be asking how come we are not feeding other countries. Independents who weren't a waste of your vote were thought to be impossible until Zali and Helen and Cathy [McGowan]. I think they were lighthouses. They showed people, oh, there are people we admire here, they're smart, they're capable, they're working in our interests and we'd like more of that, please. I don't think this movement would have happened without their lighthouse example."

RedBridge did its first benchmarks in the targeted seats in September and October 2021. The work was quantitative and qualitative, and continued through until the election. From late January, the firm was polling in the teal seats once every three or four weeks – an expensive exercise that brought the Climate 200–backed independents into major-party league in terms of resourcing.

As RedBridge entered the field, the former ABC foreign correspondent Zoe Daniel was at a professional crossroads following her return to Melbourne after covering the Trump administration in Washington. She'd left the ABC and was putting together what came next. Her friend since university days, another former ABC alumnus, the sports journalist Angela Pippos, called Daniel with a surprise. "She said, are you sitting down," Daniel says. "I said, what on earth are you up to? She said, there's this 'Voices of' thing and I have put your name forward as someone who might like to stand as an independent. I said – no way."

Daniel lives in the Victorian electorate of Goldstein, which at the time was held by the Liberal moderate (he prefers modern Liberal) Tim Wilson. Daniel thought a safe Liberal seat held by a six-year incumbent didn't look like a viable prospect. "I said no," Daniel says. "But then journalistic curiosity got the better of me and I said to Ange, let's meet with them anyway because I'm curious to see how it all works."

Fourteen people had self-nominated to run in Goldstein. The Voices of Goldstein group set up a Zoom conversation moderated by Sue Barrett, who later became one of Daniel's campaign managers. Daniel was still a no, but Barrett persisted. Daniel agreed to go through an interview. She felt that process would prove decisive once and for all, "because I had to write a whole screed about what I could bring, and then I did an interview and then the panel did a mock press conference." After that, she moved from no to soft yes. Her family was torn; husband dead against initially, "but the kids, especially my son, were advocating strongly that someone had to step up. He said this was an opportunity to do something for us."

To try to reassure herself this wasn't total folly, Daniel looked at what had happened in the state seats overlapping and adjoining Goldstein – Brighton, Sandringham, Caulfield. "It was apparent to me, looking at the previous few state elections, that those contests had been tightening," she says.

"I did say to the Voices group that I wouldn't nominate until we'd done polling. So we did polling in October 2021." Given there wasn't a candidate, RedBridge posed questions such as: if there was a candidate like Zali Steggall, would you support them if they ran in Goldstein? "The polling suggested the seat was within reach," Daniel says. At that point, she shifted from soft to hard yes.

I'm interested in her motives for entering the fray. She gives me a good answer. As you'd expect, Daniel nominates the lack of action on the climate crisis. As a foreign correspondent, she'd covered too many climate-related disasters around the world. She'd experienced the consequences of storm surges and beach erosion while on the committee of a surf club down Victoria's Great Ocean Road, and had experienced the lack of preparedness from government agencies. As a mum of a thirteen-year-old daughter, "women's empowerment is also important to me."

But years of bearing witness to Trump had also sparked a visceral concern about the state of democracy. "The overarching motivation for me has been a lack of trust in leadership," Daniel says. "Gaslighting, sometimes overt lying, the manipulation of the public, disinformation, often the poor performance of the media within that matrix, not only here – obviously I was fresh out of covering the Trump administration and the deliberate seeding of doubt that Trump did throughout his period as president, but particularly the seeding of doubt through 2020 that the election might be stolen, which then led to people storming the Capitol."

Daniel had a front-row seat to the dangerous erosion of democracy in one of the greatest countries on earth. Coming home, she didn't want to be a spectator in her own democracy. Daniel says the times we live in feel too serious to stand on the sidelines. She didn't know if she could win Goldstein, but she couldn't, in good conscience, sit it out either.

"Trust and integrity goes to all policy," Daniel says.

Let's return to election night. At Labor campaign headquarters in the city, Wayne Swan, the party president, and Paul Erickson, the campaign director, were hunkered down for a long night given the results in Western Australia would, for once, be critical. Visitors to CHQ were quarantined in a room where they could watch the results. Campaign staff, gathered in the media area, were on the Wallabys – a mouth-punching sparkling mineral water that purports to be "volcanic filtered" (whatever that means) – which had been consumed in copious quantities during the contest because Erickson had insisted CHQ remain alcohol-free. At the beginning of the contest, Erickson had read campaign staff the riot act about culture, a worthy bit of leadership given all the controversies surrounding the toxic work environment in Parliament House. But some witnesses to that pep talk found it hard to keep a straight face because the message was delivered on a karaoke microphone that was kept in the chief of staff's office. The karaoke microphone remained safely stowed on election night, even after it became clear Labor was safely on the victory path.

I was with my team in *Guardian Australia*'s head office in Sydney. I thought Morrison would win the contest narrowly. When we'd travelled to marginal seats around the country, voter reaction to the prime minister had been viscerally negative. That should have been a harbinger, or at least a clue. But I discounted the field evidence on a few fronts. Morrison had been extremely disciplined during the campaign and Albanese had stumbled several times. I had no handle on how the stumbles played with the voters we'd met around the country, who said things to us like "Albo seems a nice enough bloke, but I don't know anything about him." Surely the stumbles would have made undecided voters hesitate?

The main reason I thought Morrison would hold on despite the fear and loathing was the electoral buffer the Coalition had built up in 2019. The rout in the previous election meant Labor was very unlikely to gain any seats in Queensland. I'd visited the two marginal seats in northern

Tasmania, Bass and Braddon, just before the campaign started. They didn't feel like Labor gains to me. With zero gains in Queensland, and Bass and Braddon not in the Labor column, I couldn't find a conventional pathway to victory on the electoral map. Labor strategists in Western Australia were playing down the prospects of a landslide in the state. The wise counsel (which turned out to be expectation management – always got to watch that) was Labor might gain two seats, three if it's a great night. I had my doubts about whether Labor could pick up Boothby in South Australia. The seat was very marginal, yes, but the Liberals had always held it, and they had fielded an impressive candidate. Labor was very hopeful about gains in Sydney, but they'd been hopeful of gains in Sydney in 2019 as well and they hadn't materialised. As for the teals, I suspected Daniel would win in Goldstein because she'd run an impeccable race and Tim Wilson seemed to be doing everything he could during the campaign to hand her the seat. Wentworth also seemed likely to fall. But I suspected that would be it.

As we plugged in for election-night coverage in Surry Hills, party strategists I trust predicted the outcome would be a narrow win for Albanese, assuming Labor's private polling was reliable. But people were warning that Saturday night's count would be a roller-coaster because half of all votes had been cast before election day. No postal votes would be counted on election night. And furthermore, the local booths that were likely to be counted first would generally not be representative of the final result. The early run of results for Labor looked bad – worse than in 2019. At Labor CHQ the mood was distinctly downbeat for the first couple of hours. Glum, even. Everyone had 2019 déjà vu.

But as the night wore on, it became clearer that the seats were breaking in the right direction for Labor. As predicted, the result would be close. The positive swing in the West was sufficient to deliver four seats, Boothby had fallen, Reid and Bennelong had come through, as had Robertson on the Central Coast of New South Wales. Higgins in Melbourne had fallen to Labor. The teals had broken through everywhere – Goldstein, Kooyong, Mackellar, North Sydney, Wentworth and the blue-ribbon seat of Curtin in the west. The Greens had also surged, gaining two lower-house seats from the Liberals in Brisbane and one from Labor. The result felt like a profound correction to the 2019 election, when climate change had been a central part of the reason Labor lost, alongside confusion over its franking credits policy, which the Coalition had weaponised as a death tax.

This progressive stampede was remarkable given the verdict the country had returned only three years earlier. The Liberal Party had suffered an epochal rout in its metropolitan heartland, including losing a prime ministerial prospect in Josh Frydenberg. The crossbench was huge. Labor had reached cruising altitude and was tracking to seventy-seven seats despite not gaining any ground in Queensland. My head was struggling to process all these developments. Normally the response to a narrow major-party victory on election night would be to flick the switch instantly to punditry about the inexorable instability inside the governing party. That was Malcolm Turnbull's fate after the 2016 contest; the tight election result presaged his death by a thousand cuts. But the circumstances in 2022 were different. Labor had emerged with the magic number of seats and with a buffer of protection around Albanese's narrow governing majority – progressives in the parliament as far as the eye could see – and the Liberal Party seemingly devoid of an easy path back to majority government.

In typical journalist fashion, I swung from not seeing the result coming to imagining conspiracy. When I considered the unusual pattern of gains and losses, it looked to me as if the progressive political forces in Australia had convened a secret meeting and carved up the electoral landscape in the style of a peace treaty after a war. Australian politics is an intimate and cloistered subculture. These people are connected. They all know each other. Given the thumping electoral endorsement for the teals, it seemed to me likely independents would have picked up Higgins, Bennelong, Ryan, Brisbane and Griffith had they contested those seats. The absence of a Climate 200–backed independent had created space for Labor gains that were crucial on its pathway to victory, and the Green gains enabled the third-largest party in Australia to finally crash through in the lower house.

After the election I asked the Greens leader Adam Bandt whether there had been some top-secret progressive stitch-up that we all missed. He laughed. "There wasn't a secret meeting in a basement," he says.

Samaras says the 2022 result was a watershed, but suggests I might have seen it coming had I looked a bit closer at the results the cycle before and factored in the impact of the pandemic. "In 2019, all the trends were there," he says. "Morrison won, but he lost votes in higher-educated electorates. In Higgins, the Liberals had swings against them. In Kooyong. The patterns were there, but what the pandemic did was put it on another gear; it sped up patterns established for ten years, it accelerated the process. People lost all their patience with the political system. What would have probably occurred in another election's time happened this time."

I couldn't shake the feeling that the progressive forces in Australia must have cooked this up – there must have been extensive undeclared coordination – because the ultimate landing point was so elegant. I asked Holmes à Court why a teal independent didn't contest Higgins in Melbourne. "Our early polling showed that Higgins was the most prospective electorate for an independent," he says. "We would have loved to have seen a strong independent campaign in Higgins, but surprisingly, the community independents movement just didn't reach critical mass there. Climate 200 never started a campaign or chose a candidate; we waited for the community to come to us. I reckon an independent could have won Higgins. A missed opportunity."

He says Climate 200 didn't amble about tilting at windmills. The investments had one criterion: winnability. "It's one thing having people who want to run a campaign, but if they can't win there's little point putting resources in." Climate 200 formulated its own objectives and stuck to its knitting. "By March, our polling showed that seven independent candidates were within striking distance of winning. We reshaped our work to prioritise those candidates, and they all won," he says. "We had our head down. When we came up for air, we were very surprised by how many seats Labor and the Greens won. In aggregate it was a bloodbath."

Labor stayed in its lane. The Albanese campaign was flat-out trying to consign the Coalition to Opposition. But Labor also did nothing to impede or obstruct the independent campaigns. The Albanese campaign gave soft permission for Labor supporters to vote independent in Liberal-held seats. Labor supporters in teal-targeted seats were encouraged to vote tactically, apart from the Senate race in the ACT. A few weeks into the campaign, Labor strategists were concerned that the Climate 200–backed independent David Pocock was doing well enough to knock off the incumbent Labor senator, Katy Gallagher. Erickson dispatched Julia Gillard to tell Canberrans who liked the look of Pocock to put him second, after Gallagher. Apart from that, Labor stayed out of the way of the teal campaigns. This was an innovative campaign strategy to pursue in an age of rusting off and political atomisation: Labor, in essence, licensed a quasi-political party in Melbourne, Sydney and Perth to make the argument people could get rid of Morrison by voting for someone other than Labor.

Paul Erickson is very clear. Morrison was the most significant factor determining the ultimate election outcome. Wanting the prime minister gone created a unity ticket for voters in different geographical territories. It bridged the interests of materialists and post-materialists. "Throughout the campaign, the country's rejection of Scott Morrison remained the biggest factor for voters," he says. "A majority of voters had a negative view of him, and this was true everywhere we looked. He was as unpopular in Hunter as he was in Higgins."

While Labor did nothing to impede the teal campaigns, it would be wrong to conclude from this that Labor has now hoisted the white flag; that it no longer wants to pursue conventional strategies to boost its primary vote and govern in its own right. Quite the contrary. Strategists understand that the old red team–blue team forms of tribal allegiance being supplanted by the values-based identity politics of the digital age represents an existential threat to Australia's left–right political duopoly. Rather than accepting the inevitability of decline, rather than surrendering to the mega-trend, Labor has been relentless in chasing the means of staying alive.

After Morrison beat Shorten in the 2019 election, Samaras says, there was a "really robust discussion" in Labor ranks about viable pathways to victory because the ten-year primary-vote trend was so bad. This discussion broke cover at the end of 2019 when Daniel McNamara, an official who had worked for several years with Erickson in Labor's national secretariat, wrote an opinion piece published in *The Age* arguing that making a priority of winning back blue-collar voters in the regions – which was the strategy Fitzgibbon followed when he tried to sink Butler and Bowen's climate change policy after the 2019 rout – was "pissing into the wind."

McNamara argued Labor needed to look beyond working-class voters in the regions and build a new coalition of voters who "predominantly live in cities and their surrounding suburbs, span a range of income brackets from the precariat to the middle class, tend to work in the broad and expanding services sector, and are increasingly culturally diverse and university-educated." He foreshadowed a new Labor pathway to victory through the teal seats, noting there were "plenty of Liberal-held seats in Melbourne, Sydney, Brisbane, Perth and Adelaide which are ripe for the picking because their voters are alienated by the Liberals' drift into right-wing populism."

McNamara's public musing triggered a minor explosion inside Labor because this thinking countenanced Labor becoming a post-labour party. For many Laborites, this is absolutely unthinkable. Shedding a key part of its historical identity would have split the ALP. Some right-wingers went ballistic, assuming the piece was sanctioned kite-flying ahead of the 2022 campaign. It wasn't, and at no point did Erickson – a left-wing national secretary – signal he intended to write off traditional Labor territory when he briefed federal MPs ahead of the campaign.

Back in May 2021, Erickson scheduled a half-day session in Canberra with Labor's marginal-seat holders. At one point during the session, the right-winger Michelle Rowland, who holds the western Sydney seat of Greenway, pointed to the elephant in the room. She asked Erickson to outline Labor's pathway to victory. Erickson didn't nominate the Liberal-held inner-city seats that fell to independents in 2022. He listed fifteen or so electorates that were outer-suburban and regional. Labor's targeted voters were working people worried about cost-of-living pressures because their wages were stagnant, not the post-material equality, integrity and climate justice cohort targeted by the teals.

In a conversation for this essay, Labor's campaign director says: "Our campaign sought to grow support for Labor in territory that has traditionally been solid for us. We sought to retain the suburban and provincial marginal seats we'd won in 2016 and 2019 – places like Eden-Monaro, Dobell, Macquarie, Gilmore, Corangamite and Dunkley – and in those places we did very well. We needed to retain the Labor seats on the [NSW] Central Coast and around Newcastle and the Hunter Valley." Because of Morrison's misjudgments, other opportunities in the capital cities then opened up during the parliamentary term. "Ultimately, we gained some seats that haven't traditionally voted Labor, like Bennelong, Higgins and Boothby."

Winning majority government requires banking what you have and looking for incremental gains at every election based on the prevailing conditions. One of the prevailing conditions Labor was able to capitalise on in 2022 was Mark McGowan's popularity in Western Australia, a political ascension Morrison had helped deliver by taking pot shots at Western Australia's border closures during the pandemic. The West swinging for Labor was critical in the final seat count.

If you want to consider how these electoral imperatives manifest in policy formulation, look no further than climate change. If Labor believed it could write off its traditional territories, ignore Western Australia's long history as a resources state and form a majority government just with the electoral endorsement of post-material inner-city progressives, the 2030 emissions reduction target would likely be higher than the number put to voters in 2022. But Labor wouldn't have been able to form a majority government in 2022 if it hadn't held its blue-collar regional and outer-suburban territory. Given Queensland and northern Tasmania were a bust, it also needed gains such as Higgins, Bennelong and Boothby.

I've come to think of formulating climate policy as an exercise in swimming between the flags. There's now a bedrock of support in Australia for action within certain parameters. But Labor's view was, step outside those parameters and things start to get dangerous electorally. Labor knew 2022 would not be a replica of 2019. Business would not be out attacking the 43 per cent emissions reduction target as economy-wrecking, and Labor saw its primary vote lift after the policy was unveiled in December 2021. The campaign environment felt like tailwind, not headwind. But the goodwill wasn't infinite. Morrison spent much of his prime ministership courting voters either frightened about or opposed to the transition.

While Morrison was nibbling relentlessly at Labor's blue-collar supporters, progressive forces were also busy on the left flank. Both the Greens and the independents wanted a higher target than 43 per cent. Climate science actually demanded a higher target, but Labor's calculation was it had reached the political and practical max-out point with its policy settings. Swimming between the flags isn't a highly calibrated science – it's always a point-in-time assessment. During the campaign, strategists watched some of Labor's vote leak to the Greens. Some of that leakage reflected the lack of ambition to curb the climate crisis, and some of it reflected concern about Albanese's unsteady campaign performance.

An analysis of voting flows undertaken by the Centre for Social Research and Methods at Australian National University says the largest aggregate shift in party support between April and May 2022 was from Labor to the Greens. Three weeks from polling day, key strategists knew the Labor campaign in the Liberal-held seat of Ryan was over and the Greens would likely take the seat. Labor's shadow environment minister Terri Butler was also in trouble in Griffith. The Greens were campaigning very effectively in metropolitan Brisbane, having built a formidable ground game in the city, but the hope was Butler could hang on. In the end, she lost. With no teal in the field, the Greens also pinched Brisbane from the Liberals.

While the Greens gained two Liberal seats and one from Labor, the success of the feminised teal insurgency blew a gaping hole in the Coalition seat count. Women and urban professionals rusted off, according to post-campaign research undertaken for the Liberal Party. Coalition MPs were told in a strategy session held after the election that the Morrison campaign failed to win a majority of female voters across all age cohorts in the 2022 contest, and only 25 per cent of women voters aged between eighteen and thirty-four voted Liberal. The decade of wrecking on climate policy was one part of the problem. As well as the gender bloodbath, the Liberals also lost support from inner-city renters and urban professionals. Several Liberals also pointed to a significant backlash in the Chinese-Australian diaspora caused by Morrison and Peter Dutton's cartoonish weaponisation of the Canberra–Beijing relationship and related national security issues.

The point of stepping through all these things in such detail is to lay out all the components of the puzzle. Australians are punishing the major parties for a range of reasons. In this last election cycle, the Liberal Party was punished most of all. Some of the punishment relates to a lack of faith in probity and accountability in public life – a sense that establishment politics is more preoccupied with itself, its pork barrels and perks, jobs for the boys and girls, than with citizens. Some of the contemporary rusting off reflects people believing major parties, and the traditional, structural adversarialism of the two-party system, don't reflect their identities and values. *Why are these politicians always negative, always carping? The Liberals are too right-wing. Labor is too timid and centrist.*

Simon Holmes à Court says change is here. New politics is happening whether the major parties are ready or not. "If you look at the trends of primary vote for the two major parties, we are not far from the possibility of never having majority government again," he says. "It's foolish to predict the future in politics but maybe the last election was a lighthouse showing there is a possible future in Australia where we move to permanent minority government." But he concedes Australia's major parties will do everything possible to prevent that eventuality. Holmes à Court says he expects the post-election prognostications that happen after every cycle through the Joint Standing Committee on Electoral Matters to coalesce around "clipping the wings of the independent movement – in the same vein as Albanese's [early] staffing cut for the indies."

BIG TENTS AND UNIFYING THEORIES

Australia's major political parties are big-tent actors. Big-tent parties need to court and hold diverse electoral coalitions to form majority governments, so they have to appeal to millions of voters whose values may not align with one another. This process gets harder as people become less tolerant of opposing views. This phenomenon represents an intensifying conundrum for the major parties – how to pursue the compromises associated with big-tent politics in an impatient and uncompromising age.

While maintaining diverse electoral coalitions in an age of cancel culture is hard for contemporary major parties to manage, functional (I hope everyone caught the *functional* in this sentence) big-tent parties can be important automatic stabilisers in a democracy. To understand this point, it's useful to look to the United States. Like Australia, the US has a two-party system nominally, but there's no major-party discipline. Every vote is a free vote. Economic hardship and rampant cultural polarisation in that country have created the conditions for ratbag representatives to infiltrate the Republican Party and drag the Grand Old Party in a direction of reactionary populism – a trend that culminated in the election of a post-truth proto-fascist, Donald Trump, a president with scant respect for democratic customs and institutions. The incoming Democratic president, Joe Biden, has attempted since winning office to rebuild the political centre by having an orderly policy agenda and seeking some bipartisan cooperation to reset the political system. But he's faced resistance at every turn, and because the United States has a major-party system without major-party discipline, the president can't control his own caucus, let alone reset relationships with Republicans who believe the only path to professional advancement is exhibiting fealty to Trump or Trump surrogates. The impossibility of compromise leading to incremental but tangible progress that citizens in a democracy can rally around renders more obstructive polarisation an inevitability. This dangerous cycle feeds itself.

What functional big-tent parties do is model the reality that deliberation and compromise can lead to progress. These settlements are broad-brush by definition. Democratic parliaments are not iTunes or Spotify. Citizens can't curate their own playlists. Parliaments cannot possibly reflect the will of every individual citizen. They model the art of the possible.

By contrast, political disrupters can offer voters something more customised than diffuse major-party settlements. The currency is often empathy and validation. In the positive, disrupters mirror the gnawing hunger among engaged people for a more perfect democracy as a bulwark in uncertain and dangerous times. In the negative, the mirroring engages with voter grievance or alienation. In either case, the connection point is more bespoke. This feels attractive when the old tribalism – being born into your political allegiances – is being supplanted by cultural affinity, which is more fluid, and more acquired than predetermined.

The forty-third parliament in Australia – the first minority parliament since World War II, and the best parliament I've covered by several orders of magnitude – demonstrated that hung parliaments *can* enact an ambitious policy agenda through the cooperation of big parties, smaller parties and independents. But that level of legislative success relies on constructive relationships and goodwill. Everyone has to value getting things done. Not every minority parliament will function as cooperatively and productively as the Gillard parliament, because not everybody enters politics to get things done. These propositions aren't binary, of course. Major-party obstruction can coexist with major-party discipline, and there is a school of thought that Coalition governments – particularly Abbott's and Morrison's – existed largely to stop Labor doing things rather than to do anything much themselves.

We can summarise the swings and roundabouts this way. Some major-party actors are resisting the mega-trend of declining primary votes reflexively, because they enjoy power and want to preserve their capacity to exercise it. But others genuinely fear the consequences of an electoral realignment where Australia drifts into permanent minority governments comprised of masses of independents or fragmented bespoke political blocs more intent on narrowcasting to their voting base than achieving progress, however imperfect. For some, this feels like a recipe for roiling and stagnation that has the capacity to corrode the foundations of representative democracy.

It's not just Labor standing on this electoral faultline. The Liberal Party faces the same base erosion as Labor. Scott Morrison attempted to stave off the electoral train wreck of 21 May by pursuing a similar swimming-between-the-flags strategy on climate policy — although a more caustic observer might conclude he spent more time on the sand working on his tan than grappling with the fundamentals. Morrison persuaded the National Party to support a net-zero emissions reduction target for 2050 (genuflecting to metropolitan centre-right progressives). While shifting on 2050, he couldn't budge on 2030, so he had to concoct a nonsense. He said the 2030 target need only be a 26 to 28 per cent cut unless technological change magically yielded more significant abatement. Morrison couldn't flick the switch to science and sense because of the falsehoods he'd unleashed in 2019, including but not limited to electric vehicles representing a "war on the weekend." Voters saw through his nonsense and the Liberals were smashed. Ironically, many of the MPs who paid the price were the Liberal moderates who had led an internal campaign for stronger climate action.

While Labor has, for now at least, resolved that the only way to get a majority is to swim credibly between the flags, the Liberal Party under Peter Dutton has some very tough decisions to make over the coming three years. Does the party renounce big-tent politics and join other right-leaning narrowcasters? Recent history tells us that competent independents, once elected, can be very hard to dislodge. It's hard to see how the Coalition can form a majority government while the teal buffer persists. The opening months of Dutton's leadership suggest his inclination is to write off the inner city and come for Labor's traditional territories in the hope of pushing Albanese into minority government. But surely the Liberals would be better off trying to rebuild a diverse electoral constituency. Australia would certainly be better off if that was Dutton's approach.

Samaras says Labor's strategy for holding the shifting tectonic plates together in 2022 was outsourcing a political wedge to the teals. With the teals coming after the Liberal Party in blue-ribbon territory in the inner city, Morrison couldn't fully weaponise climate change against Labor without cruelling his own chances of holding government. Looking ahead, Samaras thinks it will be difficult for Albanese to reverse the trend of the last several federal elections, with major parties attracting a smaller share of the vote. "This notion Labor will get a honeymoon and sentiment will swing hard towards Labor at the next election? I don't reckon. Look, there might be a blip, but in terms of the trend, we are going to see the majors decline, and it will get harder and harder to form majority governments."

Erickson says lots of people will have theories about why Labor broke through in some places and not others, about whether the teals represent salvation or threat, and about what comes next.

A lot of sweeping declarations are made in hindsight, and these hindsight judgments can be disproven as early as the next election cycle. Every election has its own zeitgeist. Every cycle throws up new issues, actors and different challenges. During a campaign, strategists have information, but they don't have the benefit of knowing the result. Erickson says if you are perceptive, perhaps you see that something is happening, but "if you've got a blind spot, you might not even see it coming."

"It's a mistake to focus on one part of our coalition or one trend among many and reach grand conclusions," Erickson says. "The point of electoral coalitions is they are composed of people who don't necessarily agree on everything.

"In the main I am sceptical of unifying theories of how Labor wins. Before May this year we'd done it three times since the war, and once in my lifetime. If other people want to live by a set of rules dictated by the historical memory of 1972, 1983 and 2007, that's a matter for them, but it's not how we ran the campaign. Equally, if the media spends the next three years focusing on how the independents defeated the Liberals, they'll probably miss the real story of the next campaign until it turns up in the results."

I can understand the frustration fuelling this rebuke. The pundit complex around politics sprinted from heavily discounting the prospects of the teal insurgency to predicting the imminent demise of the major-party system. But a genuine point of interest in the independents' campaigns is what happened on the ground in those electorates. Samaras, as a long-time major-party operative, was struck by the organic voter uprising. He says Climate 200 had the resources to buy in a lot of expertise to inform their investments in the independents' campaigns, and the money professionalised the campaigns the independents ran. But he also says what happened on the ground just happened.

"People just emerged, young data-savvy professionals joined the campaign and helped at a grassroots level all the way up to data facilities helping them out, crunching the numbers we produced and using them to guide their doorknocking," he says. "They grabbed our data and paired up different styles of doorknocking campaigns. Because their volunteer base was so extensive, they were almost able to have like doorknocking on like. If the person targeted in this house was young, of a certain age group, then they would get someone of the same age to doorknock them."

Daniel was also blown away by the community response in Goldstein. "We started seeing a movement grow," she says. "People were keen to doorknock and hand out fliers or be with me at street stalls. I'd go out for a run or to walk the dog and there would be people in Zoe T-shirts. People would wind down their window and call out to me, 'Go Zoe.' There was this real sense of the community feeling like they were owning it. What was happening well overtook me. It was the community lifting me."

She says the pandemic was a significant factor delivering what felt like a people-powered revolution on the ground. "People remembered what community was like. They realised again the value of focusing on your local community and being part of your local community, because they had to be. Especially in a community like mine, I accept not everyone was living in this environment, but in bayside Melbourne, you'd smell curries cooking. All the dads would be out with their kids at the footy field. There were kids on bikes and people walking dogs and all the local cafés had people out the front chatting and that was lockdown Melbourne.

"I think that recognition, that renewed sense of community that grew out of a really negative thing, then sprouted into a positive community-led campaign," she says. Daniel had a data analyst and demographer working on her campaign who spoke about feasibility, desirability and inevitability as the three cycles. The feasibility cycle was the first campaign launch, with six or seven hundred locals. As interest grew, the campaign moved to desirability – "more people jumped on because of the desirability of what we were doing, the fun and the positive energy." The campaign hit inevitability when "so many people got involved that it felt like a rock rolling down a hill. It wasn't going to stop."

"I don't know if I ever got to the point where I thought I would win but we had a second launch right after the election was called, down on the foreshore, a beautiful blue-sky day and we had almost 2000 people in a park. That was like: woah."

A couple of political elder political statesmen, one Labor, one Liberal, looked in on proceedings, Barry Jones and Ian Macphee. "Barry Jones said to me, I've never seen anything like this in Australian politics," Daniel says. "This is something.

"Something is happening here."

THE NEW POLITICS

Something definitely happened on 21 May 2022. But the pressing question now, of course, is what happens next. What are the prospects of a new politics in Australia? Before we get to prospects, first let's consider the foundational question: what is the new politics? The erosion of the major-party system remains a trend-in-progress. In broad terms, the new politics eschews major-party custom and practice, it is bottom-up rather than top-down; new politics can be pragmatic, but the virtue it signals is idealism and aspiration; new politics champions dialogue over combat because the tone is positive; the core values are integrity, transparency.

But if our definition is to be inclusive, the new politics covers more than just progressive disruption to the red team and blue team. Australian progressives were delighted by the election outcome, pleased about Scott Morrison and major-party politics getting an uppercut, because their parliament looked more like them. But on an inclusive definition, Donald Trump is new politics. He's a classic disrupter, and a successful one. He's engineered a reverse takeover of a major political party, transforming the Republicans into a reactionary cult. To localise this question – would I be writing an essay about the new politics, would I feel like parsing the possibilities for more enlightened or creative representation if our Trump-lite, the Liberal defector Craig Kelly, who became the parliamentary leader of the United Australia Party, held his Sydney seat of Hughes instead of losing it, and was joined by several Palmerites (including Clive Palmer himself) in the House and the Senate? Would this insurgency be new politics, or would that have another label?

The point is that new politics can manifest in a variety of forms, some constructive, others corrosive. The Climate 200–backed teals have now delivered a successful prototype; a replicable and scalable political insurgency model that can be deployed by any smart activists who can raise sufficient funds to field professional campaigns powered by salient issues. Palmer has invested millions trying to lever himself and his surrogates back into a kingmaking position in our legislature. Will he now conduct a similar review to the one Holmes à Court conducted after the 2019 election? Will he undertake granular analysis to determine what he needs to change in order to break through, or will Australians be spared the consequences of an opportunistic billionaire's sudden humility and curiosity?

Given a range of actors could experiment with the Climate 200 prototype for different electoral ends, the special minister of state, Don Farrell, has already flagged his interest in legislating a cap on election spending. Labor raised the same issues after 2019, after Palmer outspent McDonald's, Toyota and Coles spruiking his United Australia in the year leading up to the 2019 federal election, and spent more than $8 million on saturation advertising in the final week of the contest. Climate 200 raised $13 million in 2022 from 11,200 donors. The Coalition wasn't interested in caps when Palmer was the problem, because he wasn't a problem for them. Now the tables have been turned, it will be interesting to see whether a new consensus emerges.

Climate 200's executive director Byron Fay told the National Press Club in July that spending caps were fine, but any restrictions like that needed to be designed carefully to "make sure we are not disadvantaging future community groups that want to put up community leaders." He added: "We should think very carefully about any reform in that space so it doesn't entrench the advantages the major parties have given themselves." By way of specifics, Fay nominated taxpayer-funded "pork-barrelling" aimed at winning votes and the $750,000 granted every three years for MPs' office expenses, including electoral communications, which Fay said were "often used for campaigning." In any case, this debate has a way to run. Right now, we can focus on the known knowns.

Australians know we need serious political representation for serious times. There is overwhelming pent-up need. We've just wasted a critical decade on climate action — a decade we can't get back. The latest State of the Environment report confirms our natural world is in crisis. Wages are stagnant. Anyone who set foot inside an emergency department during the winter knows essential services are stretched to breaking point. A whole generation will struggle to enter the housing market in the absence of the bank of Mum and Dad. Inflation is back, and that cycle may not unwind fully for a couple more years. The United States and the United Kingdom hover on the brink of recession. The pandemic isn't over, much as we'd like to pretend it is. There's an unsettling war in Ukraine and we know Australia, an Indo-Pacific middle power, sits in the hot zone of escalating great-power competition. China aspires to be the regional hegemon and our most important security partner, the United States, teeters on its post-truth cliff. What we don't know yet is whether the establishment and insurgent forces in Australia's forty-seventh parliament will work constructively together to meet the moment, or whether the most progressive parliament since 2010 will end in rancour and recrimination.

Paul Erickson has made the cut-through point that a majority of voters came together in May with a common, but negative, objective: to defeat Morrison and his government. Erickson doesn't mean this passively. Morrison was certainly the architect of his own undoing, but Labor worked to delegitimise his prime ministership by weaponising every stumble he made. That strategy was brutal and effective. It was the most effective undoing of an incumbent since Tony Abbott's assault on the legitimacy of Julia Gillard's prime ministership. But sitting on the flipside of Erickson's diagnostic is an obvious question: does Albanese have what it takes to fashion a new centre of gravity for progressivism in Australia? He won't have the cartoon villain foil of Morrison to activate voters in 2025 – although some would argue Peter Dutton offers a very salient substitute, at least in the southern states of Australia. Occupying the prime ministership on his own terms is a challenge to rise to, and a lot rides on Albanese rising to that challenge. Albanese and his cabinet have an opportunity to emerge from the electoral realignment of 2022 with the secret sauce: a positive progressive agenda capable of holding majority electoral support. Because it feels like there is a moment of genuine audacity, of creative destruction, here to capture. Australians have delivered an opportunity that politics could rise to meet.

We are very fortunate in this country. Citizens here, conscripted into cycles of political engagement by compulsory voting, have largely resisted creeping illiberal authoritarianism. Australians seem to be able to sniff out the genuine enemies of representative democracy — the sociopathic hucksters of the faux everyman political class. Voters seem to crave something real. Conspiracy and voodoo and ratbaggery are ever-present, but largely confined to the margins of our politics despite the efforts of febrile news organisations to take engagement-driving fringe attention-seeking mainstream. Incivility and rancour pound away, the lobotomising cultural thunder of our digital age. But the evidence to date suggests Australians, despite this disorienting cacophony, can remember what we are for, as well as what we are against. In 2022, a majority of Australians turned their backs on Morrison, but a central part of that rejection was an affirmation of a handful of verities, such as the need for accountability in politics, and action to address the climate crisis. But can contemporary Australian progressivism — which is now red, and green, and teal — build on this foundation? Can it mature into something that feels less protean? Or will the broad-based consensus of 2022 around climate action and a federal anti-corruption commission — notwithstanding the legitimate differences on ambition among political actors of goodwill — fracture?

What happens when the conversation reaches the gate of economic and budget reform? On the road to victory, Albanese and his colleagues were able to swim across a potential rip by focusing their economic narrative on points of agreement — the labour-market benefits of affordable childcare and the transformative benefits of a carbon-intensive economy transitioning to a renewable energy superpower. Sustained wage stagnation and high inflation has also given the Albanese government sufficient political cover to creep into once vexed policy areas, including reinstating pattern bargaining, to improve pay and conditions. But not all progressives will agree to the point of compromise when the question inevitably rolls around to: who should be taxed more and what programs should we cut? I say *inevitably*, because the federal budget is in structural deficit.

That's a problem that needs fixing. Fixing it creates losers, and the institutional interests currently intent on playing nice with Labor because they
are so relieved to see the back of Morrison will only bear so much redistribution without going to war. As we ponder what the new politics is,
we also need to wonder exactly what the new Australian progressivism
might be, whether it is resilient enough to weather familial differences,
and whether its roots are deep enough to survive any fightback from the
usual suspects.

Right at the minute, Albanese is navigating much simpler terrain. He's
where he was at the opening of the forty-third parliament, when it was
incumbent on him to prove to Tony Windsor he wasn't that smart-arse
from student politics. The priority now in Albanese's relationship with
voters is creating trust, which is why the prime minister has been focused
on the delivery of election promises. But we've already reached a tipping
point on one of those promises, the controversial 'stage three' tax cuts
due to take effect in 2024.

Labor was never comfortable with the stage three package, which costs
a bomb and predominantly benefits higher income earners. But it rolled
over pre-election because opposing the package felt too politically difficult. In the weeks before Labor's first budget in October, the government·
grappled in public with a simple question: is it worse to break this promise or keep it? Keeping the promise will blow a hole in the tax base at
a time when global uncertainties call for budgetary prudence. Conditions call for a strengthening of Australia's fiscal buffers. The treasurer
attempted to make that evidence-based case two weeks out from the
budget – his rationale being that when conditions change, smart people
change their minds. But breaking the stage three promise also triggers
questions of trust. In the end, Albanese shut down the stage three debate.
The decision was kicked down the road.

Albanese is enjoying a political honeymoon, but his prime ministership is already on the clock. Voter perceptions of prime ministers are not
formed predominantly by what leaders plan but by how they respond to

events that are unplanned. Morrison could win an election back in 2019 without a policy agenda, when nobody knew him, but not after Australians had seen him fail or flail in times of extremis. Voters will know Albanese in 2025, and they will vote on what is known.

Given progressive voters have spent three terms profoundly frustrated by a lack of action, Labor will face persistent electoral impatience. That impatience in part triggered the stage three debate – why should finite resources be allocated to income tax cuts championed by the Liberals rather than Labor priorities? Environment minister Tanya Plibersek occupies one of the portfolios where competent incrementalism won't be sufficient to allay the fears of voters animated about the climate crisis. She's not paralysed by the curse of great expectations. "I know there will be frustration and there will be some people for whom we can never do enough, but that's just life," Plibersek says. "That's being a member of the Labor Party. We choose this path, which is progress, not perfection, because when we look back, we want to be able to say we achieved this, and we achieved that, not that we held out for something that was never delivered." She adds: "I am actually really excited that the last election showed, with the teal vote, that Australians care about the environment, they care about integrity, they want to elect intelligent progressive women to the parliament. All of that for me is an unequivocal good news story."

Jim Chalmers, who carries responsibility for the economic program, and attempted to shift the goal posts pre-budget on the stage three package, says he completely understands the impatience of progressives. "I get it, after a wasted decade of missed opportunities and fucked-up Liberal and National priorities, Labor people want more and sooner to make up for lost time." Chalmers says the impatience of the base will keep Labor's feet to the fire in government, but he insists Labor's policy program in aggregate isn't incremental. Childcare. Wages policy. A resolution of the climate wars. He says this program is bigger than Bob Hawke proposed pre-election in 1983, and bigger than Kevin Rudd's pitch in 2007. Chalmers was a senior staffer during the Rudd/Gillard era. Like everyone from that period, he's thought about how you achieve change while staying in power. "My theory of governing is people will cop big things done slowly and little things done quickly, but not big things done quickly or little things done slowly.

"Governing is prioritising and sequencing and bringing people on the journey, and caring about how we best and most responsibly manage the books," Chalmers says. "Sometimes that means trade-offs and compromises and straight talk and blunt truths." Fraught, then? "A small price to pay for the privilege," he says.

If one of the tests of new politics is whether parliamentary progressives can collaborate to change the trajectory of the country, the opening sitting fortnight furnished grounds for optimism. On Thursday 4 August, I left my office in the press gallery of Parliament House and walked across to the House of Representatives chamber to watch MPs debate, amend and pass legislation giving effect to Labor's emissions reduction targets for 2030 and 2050. Having watched a lot of bad days for the climate during the amoral unhinging of the previous decade, I wanted to bear witness on the day when the Abbott era commitment of a 26 to 28 per cent cut would finally be replaced with a legislated commitment of 43 per cent by 2030.

Weeks of negotiation between Bowen and Adam Bandt had yielded a handshake on the proposal, even though the Greens wanted a higher target and a moratorium on new oil and gas developments. Hanging over the negotiations was the spectre of past disagreement between the two progressive parties which helped facilitate the climate wars. Albanese met Bowen and Bandt in his office on 1 August. The prime minister says he was clear about Labor's bottom line. Various amendments would be accepted strengthening the initial draft of the bill, but none taking Labor beyond its electoral mandate. Bandt took that back to his party the next day. Reaching consensus on the treatment of the legislation required two meetings of the Greens' party room. There was a spectrum of views, and it wasn't clear Bandt would land agreement, but he did. Bandt confirmed on 3 August that the Greens would pass the legislation in both houses.

Bowen had also engaged the teals, even though he didn't need their votes in the House. This was a gesture of consensus-building – a tacit endorsement of the mandate of the independents and an attempt to get the new progressive-leaning parliament off on the right foot.

When he managed government business in the minority parliament, the forty-third, Albanese met weekly with crossbenchers to keep Gillard's legislative program on track. Going into the forty-seventh and his first term as prime minister, Albanese says he wants to respect the input of the crossbench even though he doesn't need their numbers in the lower house. "We were happy to vote for [various amendments]," he says. "Everyone got something out of it. It was pretty positive, everyone except the Coalition, who didn't bother to move any amendments and voted against everything."

The prime minister spent the bulk of the legislative debate about the climate targets in the chamber. Because the Coalition called divisions after every amendment to record its opposition to the legislation, the chamber debate ended up spanning several hours. It's unusual for a prime minister to be in the House for hours on a frenetic parliamentary sitting day, but Albanese bunked in. Periodically he wandered up for a chat with the crossbench, then ambled back. I was curious why he stayed so long in the chamber. "Because this is important to me," Albanese says. "It was an important part of our mandate. And I think the parliament matters.

"It was also interesting to listen to some of the debate and what people were talking about," he says. "We voted for some of the amendments and we voted against some of the amendments. We knew we had the numbers, but that was an example of treating the parliament with respect. That was an important way for the government to start." Albanese is an avid student of the parliament, its standing orders and traditions. He says he could never understand Morrison's constant disparagement of him for being fluent in the customs of their shared institution. Morrison did suggest semi-regularly that Albanese's grasp of the intricacies of parliamentary procedure was evidence of deep maladjustment. "Parliament is our job," Albanese says.

THE PROMISED LAND: "A GREAT ERA OF PROGRESSIVE REFORM"

In crashing through the barrier to lower-house representation for the Greens movement, Adam Bandt has taken his political party into new territory. After years of plateau, there's been an uptick in support as voters have become increasingly alarmed about the climate crisis, and increasingly frustrated by a lack of serious action to address the threat.

Bandt entered parliament in 2010. His relationship with Albanese was formed in the crucible of the Gillard minority parliament. Some Greens consider Albanese a bête noire on principle, because he's an avid Green-slayer. The prime minister holds an inner-city electorate that the Greens have targeted for years. Albanese and his local political machine have not been afraid to be brutal in repelling these incursions. In this respect, Bandt is Albanese's mirror image, having taken the seat of Melbourne from Labor after the retirement of Lindsay Tanner, the Rudd-era finance minister. Bandt's ground machine has also proved expert in holding that gained territory against repeated Labor incursions.

When you are up to your neck in local battles to advance along the electoral map, new politics is more aspiration than practical reality. But Albanese and Bandt trust one another. Perhaps it's those commonalities, a couple of battle-hardened combatants respecting one another's technique, that scaffold their relationship of trust.

"From my side, we'll have forceful differences of opinion but I feel confident I won't be lied to," the Greens leader says of the prime minister. "To have that relationship of trust with someone in a different political party is important."

Albanese echoes the sentiment, characterising their relationship as "constructive and respectful."

While trust feels like a solid foundation for a newer style of politics, the incentives for these two leaders are mixed. At one level, this parliament succeeding and being seen to succeed would likely consolidate the position of both parties because there would be little buyers' remorse on the part of voters. But the two parties remain in direct competition for progressive votes. If Albanese and Bandt can't maintain common ground because common ground is inconsistent with their respective ideologies or their partisan objectives, the flipside of détente is weaponising failure to their own advantage. If we can't have progress, we can have product differentiation.

Labor wants to go on governing in majority. The Greens' position is maximised through minority governments in both houses. The realpolitik is that Bandt's growth strategy for the Greens is enhanced if Labor falls short of spearheading desirable action. If Labor got everything right, the Greens would have no call to action. For reasons we've outlined in detail, Labor still requires a diverse voter coalition to form majority government, while the Greens' constituency has more uniform interests. Greens voters want ambitious action on climate change. High emissions reduction targets, consistent with climate science. An end to fossil fuels. Full stop. The end. The Greens party is not attempting to form a majority government, or win or hold seats in coal districts as well as the inner city. The idealism of the Greens is also an important connection point in recruitment drives with young progressive voters. Idealism always needs a counterpoint. There are no idealists without sellouts.

Bandt started out in Labor and has kicked around hard-left politics since his teens. He's smart. He's a good communicator. He knows how to frame a cut-through argument. He says the forty-seventh parliament could be "a great era of progressive reform," but that Albanese will ultimately decide whether that potential is reached or not. "I think one of the lessons from the climate negotiations is the only limit on more progressive action is Labor's ambition," Bandt says. "So far, I would say the government is busy but timid. There are things the Greens want to get done and there are things the government wants to get done, and we would hope that the government is prepared to work with us on things we want to progress. Whether they do or not is something that's an open question for this government. The ball will be predominantly in the government's court."

I'm curious to know his benchmark for success, because Greens have different views about how to make change. Some champion the permanent campaign – consciousness-raising that remains distinct from political structure. Others want practical action. What is success in this term? Is it pushing Labor beyond its electoral mandate, to places it will struggle to go? Or is it increments of progress?

"For me, the measure of success is getting action on the inequality and the climate crisis," Bandt says. "We've got some very clear views about how to do that: keep Australia's progressive tax system, get dental into Medicare, have free childcare, and also stop opening new coal and gas."

"The government has its own priorities but there is potential for overlap. Where there's potential for overlap, we want to see action. That might mean we get a little bit less than our policy position, but it's got to mean the government does a little bit more than the policy position it took [to the election], otherwise we are not going to tackle the climate and inequality crisis.

"This was a very significant election result for us," Bandt says. "To have our vote go up during a change-of-government election and to have the incoming government's vote go down and to have more Greens and progressive voices in parliament than ever before for us signals there's a real opportunity to take action on those sorts of things."

He says the Greens fully intend to push Labor beyond its comfort zone over the next three years, but he says trust and collaboration also matter given voter frustration with the limits of political action. He says: "Having a good working relationship with the government is important to ensuring not only that we get action on those things, but for the public to know that reform is possible."

Bandt says it should be possible, with a bit of goodwill, for both parties to quarantine their respective partisan interests during governing seasons. He says the Greens will continue to try to take territory in federal elections. There will be no armistice. But when those contests are done, and the results are in, it needs to be possible to govern, and that necessitates "sitting down and have a clear-eyed understanding about where each of us is coming from."

From where Zoe Daniel sits, the opening sorties of the new parliament have been constructive. She says Labor engaged extensively on the climate bill and the proposal to establish a National Integrity Commission. During this acclimatisation phase to her new political life, Daniel is still processing information with a journalist's eye. Through that lens, pondering the prospect of a new politics, she notes that Labor needs to be "seen to be treading their own path, and not pandering to the crossbench, and they have to be seen to be not giving in or changing undertakings they made before the election because of so-called pressure." But Daniel wonders if there's a way to get past the backflip trope. "The language is always negative," she says. "I would love to think we could get to the point where the prime minister could say, I changed my mind because circumstances shifted."

Daniel thinks Labor is going to have to grapple more fundamentally with whether or not voters are sick of the reductionist nomenclature and binary, boorish culture of "old politics." She thinks the public is ready for a new style of consensus leadership in Canberra. She thinks Albanese sees that bigger picture and is grappling with it, "but the interesting dynamic for me is you've got a lot of long-term politicians there on the Labor side so used to doing things one way."

"It must feel quite unnatural for them, to try and take point-scoring out of it, to try and look at it as having productive conversations and collaborate, let's not chalk up every amendment as a win or a loss, for example," she says.

Daniel returns to the climate bill to explain her point. "From the crossbench perspective, the amendments that went through on the climate bill, I think that was seen as a successful start, a good start, but I don't think any of us would chalk that up as 'we beat Labor on that.'" She says she's entered public life with the view that moving forward with compromise is always better than being stuck, which is a different mindset than tabulating wins and losses. Daniel says what the government did on the climate bill, and what it's working towards on the anti-corruption commission, shows "strength on the government's part, not weakness."

Daniel is already starting to think ahead to the next parliament. Given Labor's "skinny" majority, she thinks Albanese needs to play the long game. Throwing forward to the next electoral contest in 2025, she notes "there's relationship-building going on now that could well become very critical in the next parliament."

This is an interesting point. The teal independents all represent seats that have been held historically by the Liberal Party. It was a matter of some conjecture in the run-up to the 2022 election whether the independents would support Morrison or Albanese in the event of a hung parliament, because the MPs would be caught between their commitment to climate action and an anti-corruption commission and the expectation of some constituents that they should support a Liberal government ahead of a Labor one.

Because Albanese got to seventy-seven seats, the teals were spared the downside risks of definitional choices. Superficially, this was a disappointment because the MPs could have maximised their positions as kingmakers in a minority parliament, as Tony Windsor and Rob Oakeshott did in the forty-third. But if the local backlash Windsor and Oakeshott faced for supporting a Labor government rather than the Coalition remains a reliable guide, the teals are lucky to have been given the opportunity of establishing themselves before having to alienate a chunk of their constituents.

The teals can rely on Albanese to treat them respectfully, and keep them in the public eye, which keeps them relevant in the eyes of voters, given the teal buffer benefits Labor electorally by making it harder for the Liberals to get to seventy-seven seats. But again, the electoral incentives are a bit mixed. Albanese needs to remind swinging voters in Liberal heartland that a vote for a climate-focused independent isn't a wasted vote, but he certainly doesn't want Labor voters in Labor-held seats defecting if new teals run against his incumbents in 2025, which seems possible, if not probable.

Albanese balancing his relationships with progressive actors in the forty-seventh parliament is a bit like Goldilocks contemplating her morning porridge. Not too hot, not too cold. Hmm. Just right.

Daniel would say this, of course, but she thinks minority parliaments are pragmatic, not unstable or obstructionist. She says she will always take progress ahead of being stuck. Daniel's point is that the current parliament provides an opportunity for everyone to prove their worth to the voters looking for new politics. If the majors, micros and independents are able to demonstrate that a group of people who don't always agree can work together without point-scoring, "then you can have minority government that is workable, particularly when the group on the cross-bench are not putting forward spurious amendments and twisting things to make a point, but are trying to deliver good policy without unintended consequences, and progress things to make things better." As for concerns about institutional dysfunction accompanying the disintegration of the major-party lock on parliamentary deliberation, she notes there are plenty of respectable democracies around the world that function perfectly well with rolling coalitions of the willing. "Countries in northern Europe do it."

Bandt stays in our hemisphere for his glass half-full. "The New Zealand experience with Jacinda Ardern was one where she cooperated with the Greens and they both saw their vote go up," he says. The Greens leader thinks New Zealand provides a workable template for progressive cooperation creating further electoral success for all the actors. For readers unfamiliar with the sequence, Ardern needed support from the Greens and New Zealand First to form her first government in 2017. Both the Labour and Greens votes went up at the 2020 election and Ardern was able to form government in her own right – a black swan event under the country's mixed-member proportional voting system. But she chose to appoint Greens to her ministry under a cooperation agreement between the two parties.

Bandt is speaking in generalities, not specifics. He doesn't mention that at the time we speak for this essay, one of the Greens Ardern put in her ministry after the last election as a gesture of cooperation is under attack from the base of his own party for being Labor-lite. Earlier this year, the New Zealand climate minister James Shaw lost the support of his party membership because he was seen as too moderate. Shaw faced the risk of losing his position as co-leader of the Greens because some of the base objected to the compromises associated with being in power. As he put it to local media, the internal tension was a "theory of change question." Some Greens thought the party was better off critiquing power than exercising it. Obviously, circumstances are different here. Albanese has not offered the Greens any ministries. There is no cooperation agreement or coalition, formal or otherwise.

But I am curious about how supporting Labor's emissions reduction targets legislation has gone down with the Greens base, given the party and the environmental movement supports significantly higher ambition. Is the Australian base now up for compromise? Hasn't that been a flashpoint in the past? Might he find himself under fire from the base if he's too friendly to Albanese?

Bandt reports, so far, so good. "The feedback has been really positive," he says. "People are happy that we've taken a small step towards progress, but people are also clear that this is round one. What the safeguard mechanism does about coal and gas, and whether we get a climate trigger ... the big pushes are still to come. People are broadly happy with where we are at."

Quite apart from the threat of any epochal electoral realignment, there are plenty of challenges for the new Labor government to manage. Senior officials say the Morrison government effectively pulled up stumps during its last months in office. A number of hard decisions were left to the new arrivals. Then there are the economic headwinds — the risk of the third global downturn in fifteen years — a downturn triggered by an inflation shock. High inflation makes it extremely difficult for a political party that ran on promises of ending wage stagnation to deliver on that promise. There's the poison pill of having to end a cut in fuel excise, pushing petrol prices up at a time when the cost of living is surging across the board. Labor has now legislated an emissions reduction commitment in advance of securing the suite of climate policies required to fulfil that commitment.

As well as attempting to turn around a decade of atrocity in climate policy, Albanese has taken on the task of enshrining an Indigenous Voice to Parliament even though it's unclear whether the Liberal and National parties will lend bipartisanship to the exercise. I wonder whether it's possible to achieve the necessary double majority if Peter Dutton decides to say no. Albanese says he hopes that won't be the case, but if it is, he'll work on building the necessary coalitions to get the referendum across the line.

"I think there are a range of people across the political spectrum who will vote yes and support the referendum," he says. "If you go outside the political parties, it's clear that an overwhelming majority of businesspeople are supportive and the peak organisations, it's clear that the churches are supportive, there's a range of non-government organisations and civil society groups who are supportive. The union movement is supportive, and all the premiers are supportive.

"I'm hopeful as many people as possible in the federal parliament support this. It's clear that a majority in the House of Representatives and the Senate will support it. I hope there's as broad support as possible. What I'm trying to do is to lead by advancing what a question and a constitutional amendment would look like without being too prescriptive – to give people space, so this isn't my proposal. I want this to be Australia's proposal going forward."

Progress on climate and a Voice to Parliament would be significant first-term Labor achievements in the event Albanese can manage all the moving parts and balance the public's appetite for vision with the very real material concerns Australians are facing in the form of higher prices and borrowing costs. Sometimes lost in the arguments about whether emissions reduction targets are ambitious enough is the reality that a revolution is already underway, and that revolution forms the spine of Labor's economic thinking. Australia's energy grid is being transformed by cheaper renewables and that trend will be supercharged by policies such as Rewiring the Nation, assuming there is sufficient skilled labour to build the required new transmission infrastructure. Coal is on the way out. Labor is inching towards having a concrete strategy to drive electrification in the vehicle fleet, pushing Australians past their range anxiety and consigning Morrison's "war on the weekend" to history. And the government is attempting to steer that profound revolution, walking quickly while keeping extravagant gestures to a minimum, in the middle of a global energy crisis sparked by Russia's brinkmanship, and with the threat of major-economy recession hovering in the background. Chris Bowen says he sought the climate portfolio because he wanted to help drive a huge structural transformation. Climate policy to his mind is the spine of the Albanese government's economic agenda. The transition to low emissions in a carbon-intensive economy like Australia's is a present-day industrial revolution. He says his objective in the portfolio is to get the transition right. Bowen understands that Labor's program is characterised by some progressives as insufficiently ambitious, but to him "this is the equivalent of Hawke and Keating dealing with falling national income."

"Don't underestimate his ambition for the country and his ambition for reform," Wong says in response to a question about what sort of prime minister Albanese will be. "He will be pragmatic, he will be sensible and he will be smart. He's never been a Don Quixote in his life, but he is ambitious about delivering change. I think people have underestimated him his whole life."

I suspect that's true, but there are two things I wonder about. The first is whether Albanese will hold to the lessons about collaborative leadership he absorbed over the past three years, or whether the lone wolf will return. I look to Katy Gallagher for advice on this question.

"He's a crafty devil," she says, with a twinkle of genuine affection. The finance minister says Albanese will try to avoid making random captain's calls that catch them all by surprise, but there might be the odd slippage along the road.

Gallagher says as a veteran of the Rudd–Gillard civil war, collegiality, trust and decent process matter to Albanese, and to all of them, so he will try very hard to be a good chairman of a good government where esprit de corps has an intrinsic value. "He's been very firm about proper process, time for proper consideration, all views expressed, that kind of stuff."

The second thing I wonder about relates to Gallagher's point about learning from the past. Albanese wants to play a long game rather than startle the Australian people with an ambitious agenda that disintegrates into chaos and is erased by Labor's political successors. Young Albanese brimmed with frustration, but the Albanese who currently occupies the Lodge believes that progress is achieved by patience and persuasion, not by haste, brute force and rampant polarisation. Morrison once declared he wasn't interested in leaving a legacy. That's all Albanese wants to do. That instinct speaks to caution.

In the final conversation we have for this essay, Albanese is in Sydney. He's on the phone. I can hear bustle in the background. A staffer arrives with documents he needs to sign. Toto goes into raptures as Albanese's son Nathan arrives for dinner.

He's settling into the rhythms of the job. During the opening couple of months, you could see him mentally pinching himself – the first press conference he fronted in the Blue Room at Parliament House. Meeting Joe

Biden. Walking up the forecourt of the presidential palace in Jakarta. Is this real? Am I here? Is this happening?

Albanese cycles between humblebrag and humility. It's his thing. It is possible to plan minutely for an ambition to be realised, be confident you've done everything possible to achieve the goal and still be astonished you've pulled it off. In the last budget reply speech Albanese delivered before the election campaign – his last parliamentary set piece as Opposition leader – I sat above him in the press gallery in the House of Representatives. As he entered the chamber, he took in his surroundings, and assessed what he was lacking. He had a speech, which he'd rehearsed and would deliver down to the footnotes, but what he lacked was joy. This could have been Albanese's last big outing in public life. He wanted atmosphere. He wanted a sense of the stakes.

Albanese looked up to the public galleries. He swung his arms, rotating from the shoulder like an Olympic swimmer about to climb onto the starting block, expelling the tension from his body. Then he signalled up to the visitors – give me something. Come on. Give me some love. Labor always packs the public gallery for budget replies, and the true believers let out a whoop and a holler for the man they hoped would lead them out of the wilderness, and gave him a rapturous endorsement at the end.

Nothing's real unless Albanese feels it. He can't just know it. On that night, he was in the moment, he'd done the homework, ticked all the boxes, but he needed to feel it, the potential victory, the possibility that he could have dragged himself relentlessly through hostile territory, performing a multiplicity of minute calculations, oscillating between ruthlessness and fealty, to the pinnacle of power in Australia. He needed to feel where the people were. "It's the gut thing: he does get where people are," Wong says. "He doesn't need a group to tell him or polling to tell him, he sort of gets where people are."

At the time we speak, Albanese is nudging his government's first 100 days. "My view is in the first 100 days of the government, what you can do is set the tone for how you intend to govern," the prime minister says.

"I believe we've done that. We've been respectful but determined. We've been clear in our objectives in dealing with the crossbenchers, and the Opposition for that matter. We've been straight about what we want. That's how I deal with people."

Does he feel the electoral ground shifting beneath his feet? Is there a new politics earthquake, and if there is, what might that mean for Labor? Albanese says society is changing. His own journey from houso to the Lodge proves that point. "It used to be if you were born into a working-class family in a unionised job, the idea was your children would also be union members, leave school and often go through a similar career path to what your parents and grandparents did," he says. "It's very different now. There's social media, there's the changing nature of society, the success of Labor in the past meant there is far more mobility across class than there was in previous generations."

Albanese says responding to what voters want from their representative democracy in 2022 is a first-principles proposition. Start by being a good government, with decent process. Start by being a prime minister elected by the people of Australia rather than installed in a party-room coup. "How you get there is important because it changes the dynamic," Albanese says. Start by valuing the parliament and the diverse representation the people of Australia have voted for. Show the people of Australia what inclusive, stable, majority government can deliver by articulating a plan and hugging your mandate. Define the deficiencies of the alternative.

Two things are observable about this government: they are cracking on with their agenda. And Albanese is also concentrating on delegitimising the Morrison era with a level of attention that incoming Labor governments generally lack. He's already rehearsing the pitch for 2025. "I'll be standing and saying we had this agenda: action on climate, economic growth, new industry, skills, aged care, cheaper childcare, cheaper medicines, advancing gender equality, Voice to Parliament," Albanese says. "This is a significant agenda and Australia needs stable government going forward."

"Our opponents are unstable, even when, on the outside, they appeared to be more stable than during the Abbott years. It's very clear Morrison was held in contempt by a vast number of colleagues, there were differences between the Liberals and the Nationals. People didn't even know who the ministers were. Their economic credibility is damaged by the debt and not having enough to show for it. The social policy agenda is damaged by gender issues and no advancement of the Voice. Childcare, aged care – no advancement, and on the environment and climate, the record is diabolical."

How do you deal with the threat of independents running in government seats in 2025? "You respect people who vote for minor parties and we've respected that, but we will argue our case," Albanese says. "You don't win people back to the Labor Party by saying minor parties get it wrong, you put your case why people should vote Labor."

Albanese brings the tutorial close to home. "In my seat, Labor's primary vote in state elections if you look at the figure last time, it's under 30 per cent. I got 54 per cent. Why? Because I argue the case for a vote for Labor. You need a government to get things done.

"I think people have been very frustrated with the political system and process, and why wouldn't they be? I think we can have something better." We need enough of a good thing, but not too much, in other words. He says there are quality independents in the parliament but "as much as every individual might be a good person, imagine what a parliament of 150 individuals would be like?"

Now, of course Albanese would say all these things. Even if he feared the era of major-party government was over, he'd avoid making that concession at all costs. But I think Australia's thirty-first prime minister senses there is a big-tent moment out there to be captured if Labor can govern competently, keep being inclusive, and avoid implosion.

That's his intuition. Competence and a bit of emotional intelligence might turn the thing.

Albanese thinks after ten years of dog-whistling substituting for progress, people want government to work. The path to boosting Labor's primary vote is give people something to vote for.

That's new politics for Albanese. Same as the old politics, before the old politics lost its way.

Albanese is only the fourth federal Labor leader to win from Opposition since World War II, but he thinks that can change. "I see Labor as the natural party of government," he says. History would say otherwise. But it's the future Albanese has his eye on. "We are the political movement that represents national progress and we represent the interests of the vast majority of Australians," he says. "We can work with business and unions. We respect First Nations people and multicultural communities. We embrace the diversity of Australia as a strength. We want to stand up for national security, not in a narrow way but in a way that promotes peace and security, including that climate change is part of security. We don't see it in a narrow way. We have an opportunity to really drive that home and to say, come the next election, if you want that to continue, vote Labor."

He suspects Australians want to be part of something: a story of recovery and rejuvenation. Audacious, seeing the green shoots of recovery in major-party end times. Quite the flex. It would require the substance to align with the rhetoric, though. It would require the Labor Party not to devour itself and throw away government.

"There's a plan," Albanese says. "There's always a plan."

I can imagine the look of satisfaction that drifts across his face. I can't see his face – we are in different cities – but I hear it in his voice. I know the look. *Keep them dancing.* Catch me if you can.

SOURCES

18   Uren disagreed: Tom Uren, *Straight Left*, Random House, 1994, p. 203.

22   "maintained closer links": Andrew Leigh, "Factions and fractions: A case study of power politics in the Australian Labor Party", *Australian Journal of Political Science*, vol. 35, no. 3, 2000, pp. 427–48.

22   brought power tools to the party office: Karen Middleton, *Albanese: Telling it straight*, Penguin Random House, 2016, pp. 231–4.

27   "throughout my leadership": Julia Gillard, *My Story*, Random House Australia, 2014, pp. 322–4.

29   But as the Melbourne political columnist: Shaun Carney, "Albanese may not inspire hope, but he knows how to hold on to leadership", *The Sydney Morning Herald*, 26 May 2021.

56   Research by the Parliamentary Library: Scott Bennett, "The decline in support for Australian major parties and the prospect of minority government", 16 February 1999, Parliamentary Library.

57   "may have ushered in": Nicholas Biddle and Ian McAllister, "Explaining the 2022 Australian Federal Election Result", Australian National University Centre for Social Research and Methods, 20 June 2022.

69   rusting off: See Gabrielle Chan, *Rusted Off: Why country Australia is fed up*, Vintage Australia, 2018.

70   "pissing into the wind": Daniel McNamara, "Labor, stop chasing the blue-collar regional mirage, your future is in the cities", *The Age*, 27 December 2019.

72   an analysis of voting flows: Biddle and McAllister, 2022.

95   better off critiquing power: Thomas Coughlan, "On the tiles: James Shaw on losing the co-leadership and advice from Metiria Turei", *The New Zealand Herald*, 26 August 2022.

Nyadol Nyuon

A majority of US Republican nominees running for the House, Senate and key state offices this year are election deniers. Most are expected to win. This will place some in positions where they can refuse to enforce election results. The threat is not theoretical. This year the Democratic secretary of state for New Mexico had to get a court order to enforce the election result of a primary.

And it gets worse. Republican lawmakers are proposing and enacting laws to restrict voting. *The Washington Post* reports that these voter restriction laws would "strain every available method of voting for tens of millions of Americans, potentially amounting to the most sweeping contraction of ballot access in the United States since the end of Reconstruction." And this is only what is happening on the political front.

On the cultural front, conservatives in the United States, sometimes backed by wealthy individuals and groups, are banning from schools books focused on race, LGBTQ+ issues or marginalised communities. Some of the books banned include biographies of Rosa Parks, Dr Martin Luther King Jr and Ruby Bridges. Ruby Bridges was the six-year-old first grader who walked through an angry mob to desegregate a school during the civil rights movement. For her protection, she was escorted by four federal marshals. The white crowd, mostly adults, were there to protest her presence. They screamed insults and racial slurs at the six-year-old. A woman held up a miniature coffin with a black doll in it. Today, some believe teaching this history is "woke," in the pejorative sense of the word.

Yet Waleed Aly and Scott Stephens' essay leaves the impression that cancel culture and political correctness pose a symmetrical threat, or an even greater threat, to American democracy than Republican attacks on voting rights. Others have arrived at the same conclusion about the essay. Ryan Cropp, an historian, writes in *Inside Story* that although the authors have no sympathy with the right wing of American politics, they advance a narrative that suggests "the fascist inclinations and genuine illiberalism of the new American right has its mirror on the left, in the form of cancel culture and political correctness."

That claim is obviously ridiculous to many, including Francis Fukuyama. Fukuyama plainly states in his book *Liberalism and Its Discontents* that the "threats to liberalism are not symmetrical. The one coming from the right is more immediate and political; the one on the left is primarily cultural and therefore slower acting."

Turning to substantive matters, I think the essay also echoes the historical justifications used to restrain and even reverse progress, especially as demanded by the historically marginalised (the contemned). This is apparent in the authors' use of language such as the "hard labour of patient appeal" or the value of maintaining hope "in the moral possibilities of persuasion." Importantly, this language is exclusively directed at the contemned. It defines what the authors deem to be the morally permissible response the contemned should have for their contemnor. There is no equivalent analysis of the contemnor's moral responsibility or whether they share any moral accountability. What is clearly argued is that responding to contempt with contempt is morally wrong. By framing the issue in this manner, the authors impose an order that treats the reaction to an issue as the issue.

To set the scene, the authors indicate there is something amiss about our time. They say we may live in the first period of history where every demographic feels "existentially slighted all the time." This has created a cycle of mutual condemnation, which leads us to treat each other with contempt. The authors argue that "democracy cannot survive contempt." All these statements are debatable.

Arguably, democracy was "born" with contempt that was visceral and violent. Women, enslaved black people and Native Americans were not equal human beings or citizens. And these groups' fights for equality always generated tensions as disruptive as in our time. The southern slave states felt "existentially slighted" enough to go to war over their right to own other humans. During the civil rights movement, white people felt "violated and victimised" by black people's demands for equality. You cannot look at the photographs or footage of violent attacks on peaceful protesters – or of the group screaming at six-year-old Ruby Bridges – without sensing that these are people who felt threatened in some fundamental manner. Dr Martin Luther King Jr, concerned by the backlash, warned that America "may now be in ... an era of change as far-reaching in its consequences as the American Revolution." Conceivably then, the existence of anger, or contempt, has accompanied the democratic experiment and isn't distinctive to our times.

An understanding that democracy was "born" with contempt shapes and redirects our attention to what should be considered a critical threat to democracy.

According to Jan-Werner Müller, a political philosopher from Princeton, what really threatens democracy isn't disagreement, since the true function of democracy is allowing for "disagreement in perpetuity." The real threat to democracy is an attack on the means or the infrastructure established for dealing with disagreements. For Müller, Crop writes, "you cannot expel or disenfranchise citizens, or attempt to limit their participation in the political process. This is democracy's 'hard border': cross it, and you pose a threat to democracy itself." That would be what the Republicans are currently doing or attempting to do, as discussed. The authors are silent on this point.

This silence might be explained by their preference for Alexis de Tocqueville's "soaring vision" of a thick democracy over a thin democracy. To the authors, thin democracy "connotes very little indeed: regular free and fair elections, the rule of law, tolerance of opposition political parties, and a set of rules that determine how publicly binding decisions get made." It is difficult, however, to see how one can achieve a version of thick democracy without first protecting thin democracy. Without thin democracy, you return to a system of institutional contempt. In any case, it has never been the lack of a "soaring vision" that is the problem. After all, the "magnanimous vision" – "we hold these truths to be self-evident, that all men are created equal" – was stated by men who, in the words of David Livingstone Smith, "participated in the brutal and degrading institution of slavery."

Nevertheless, accepting the argument that democracy cannot survive contempt, let's examine the nature of the contempt deemed to be the problem. The authors state that "contempt has been almost universally condemned as the kind of moral emotion from which nothing good can come." Immanuel Kant's moral theory of contempt provides the reasons for the universal objection. According to the authors, Kant is against contempt because "humans have an inalienable dignity simply by virtue of being humans." As such, contempt – judging "something to be worthless" – denies human beings the respect owed to them as human beings. Kant admits someone might have inward contempt, but performing that contempt outwardly is an "offence." At this stage we get the first distinguishing characteristic of contempt: it is performative. The authors distil two more: it is judgmental and comparative. We therefore get two overall statements about contempt. It is universally condemned and, distilled, it has three characteristics. Next, Aly and Stephens present three types of contempt: patronising contempt, visceral contempt and moral contempt. The authors concede these types are "not mutually exclusive" and each can "easily bleed into and inflect the others."

Considering the statement that contempt is universally condemned, that it has three characteristics, and that there are three types of contempt (which are not mutually exclusive) raises some absurd scenarios. Michelle Mason, who advances the view that contempt can be morally required in certain circumstances, probes these scenarios. She asks: if remorse were to be expressed by perpetrators of the Holocaust, ought the victims and survivors forgive such perpetrators? "Should they feel morally pressured to stifle their contempt?" These are, of course, difficult questions, but *Uncivil Wars* is meant to be addressing difficult moral issues.

Importantly, I think Mason's questioning might expose an assumption in Kant's moral theory of contempt. While Kant formulated these egalitarian principles, he himself endorsed racism and sexism. He considered black people to be unable to govern themselves, and thus they "serve only as slaves." The point isn't the racism or the sexism. It is whether Kant's theory of contempt was "tested" against those he considered less than human – in the way Mason's probing challenges us to do. It is likely Kant's theory was intended to manage relations between individuals who mutually recognise each other's humanity. This seems logical. In this situation, contempt – if allowed to fester – would threaten that mutuality and undermine the foundation of their shared life. To the contrary, where such mutual recognition doesn't exist, it is manifestly absurd to argue that enslaved people have a moral obligation or duty not to hold their enslavers in contempt because they are human beings with inalienable dignity and shouldn't be treated as worthless, while that is precisely how the enslaved are treated.

Whatever absurdities might arise, the authors appear to imply that upward contempt will always remain morally objectionable. To develop this argument, they supplement the Kantian view of contempt with their construction of a "Baldwinian" approach. This is meant to address two things. First, to embed their argument that responding to contempt with contempt isn't morally justified and should be resisted. This means that even if grave injustices exist (as they did during the civil rights movement), upward contempt is still morally objectionable. Second, the Baldwinian approach is regarded as appropriate for our time. The authors posit that in our current political environment, "in which everyone claims to be victimised, 'upwardness' becomes far from straightforward." To draw out this complexity, the authors provide the example of working-class white people who consider discrimination against them to be just as bad or even worse than that experienced by racial minorities (such as African Americans). The Baldwinian approach is advanced as providing the morally acceptable response to these challenges. In my view, however, the authors overstretch Baldwin's work.

The authors cast Baldwin's body of work as a "monument to the refusal of contempt." In addition to extracting from Baldwin's novel *Tell Me How Long the Train's Been Gone*, the authors focus on the letter in his book *The Fire Next Time*. They draw attention to Baldwin telling his nephew that he must not only accept white people, but also accept them with love because "these innocent people" are "still trapped in a history which they do not understand." The authors claim this language captures Baldwin's "moral claims for racial justice" and that it is "far removed from a disposition of contempt." The authors imply Baldwin's understanding is shared by the "greatest advocates for racial justice." These include W.E.B. Du Bois and Martin Luther King Jr. For emphasis, the authors contrast Baldwin's perception of the Black Power movement. They argue that for Baldwin the problem wasn't that "Black Power is immoral on account of its militancy." Instead, "Baldwin regarded the Black Power movement as a kind of tragic figure."

It is questionable whether Baldwin's use of phrases such as "innocent people," "accept them with love" or "war between brothers" means what the authors claim. Baldwin considered innocence, especially this particular kind of white innocence, to be a crime. Earlier in the letter quoted by the authors, Baldwin wrote: "it is not permissible that the authors of devastation should also be innocent. It is the innocence which constitutes the crime." He did not speak of innocence in the manner that we would look at a child's mistake as rendering them guiltless. This kind of white innocence is complicit, through ignorance, wilful blindness or tacit justification of the destruction of black lives. Indeed, before naming that innocence a crime, Baldwin wrote in the same letter: "I know, which is much worse, and this is the crime of which I accuse my country and my countrymen, and for which neither I nor time nor history will ever forgive them, that they have destroyed and are destroying hundreds of thousands of lives and do not know it and do not want to know it." As such, what the authors derive from this term seems to be the exact opposite of its intended meaning. In fact, it is arguable that the white working class who believe they are suffering discrimination equal to or greater than black people today, are suffering from this kind of white innocence.

Further, Baldwin's concept of love was directly opposed to the romanticised version. In *Down at the Cross*, he wrote: "I use the word 'love' . . . not in the infantile American sense of being made happy but in the tough and universal sense of quest and daring and growth." It is easy to discern how that concept of love connects with the concept of innocence: they both call for maturity. Part of that maturity is the ability to face the truth and the suffering that may bring. For Baldwin, "people who cannot suffer can never grow up, can never discover who they are." It is also debatable whether Baldwin's reference to "brother" has the implied meaning advanced by the authors. This was not necessarily a spiritual or political brotherhood; it was literal. He often referred to the rape of enslaved women and how that had led to African Americans who were "visibly and legally" descendants of enslavers. To Baldwin, black and white Americans were "blood" brothers who could do nothing to change that.

Overall, it is even harder to reconcile the authors' construction of the Baldwinian approach with the purpose of his work. Baldwin dismissed the "sloppy and fatuous nature of American good will." He claimed it could never be relied on to deal with hard problems – only with those changes born of political necessity, and by necessity he meant "concession made in order to stay on top." On the other hand, Baldwin saw no real improvements without "radical and far-reaching changes in the American political and social structure." As did King. Those who study his philosophical theory argue King's "political hopes" were informed by the conviction that societies have to "grow and change, in radical and perhaps revolutionary ways," to achieve justice.

This call for "radical and far-reaching changes" seems to go against much of what the essay advocates, and directly contradicts the authors' characterisation of the Baldwinian approach as being about "steadfastness and patience." Baldwin's approach couldn't be more different. In 1971, speaking of his two-year-old nephew, Baldwin said his frame of reference was that his nephew was not going to live the life he had lived even if it "demands blowing up the Empire State Building or whatever it demands." He is known to have asked white America how much more time it needed for its progress when it had already cost his father and him time. He reproached William Faulkner for similar reasons, stating the time Faulkner asked for "does not exist." For Baldwin there was no time in the future; the time was "always now."

Arguably, King also rejected calls for patience. In his memoir *Stride Toward Freedom*, King mentions a speech in which he told the congregation that they had come "to be saved from that patience that makes us patient with anything less than freedom and justice." Famously, King reproved the well-intentioned white moderate who was more devoted to "order than to justice; who prefers a negative peace which is the absence of tension to a positive peace which is the presence of justice." He said he had "almost reached the regrettable conclusion" that these well-intentioned moderates were a greater stumbling block to black people's stride to freedom than the Ku Klux Klan. With these counterarguments laid out, it is difficult to reconcile the authors' construction of Baldwin's, and by extension King's, position with their own.

And this is not their only error. The authors also misunderstand Baldwin's critique of what they call the "Black Power movement." Perhaps they meant the Black Panther movement. Black power is a concept that has militarist and non-militarist expressions. It can simply mean pride in blackness or culture. In the cultural sense, it is a way of shoring up a feeling of self-worth against the many racial stereotypes black people often confront. Black Power can, indeed, have militaristic and supremacist expressions. The Black Panther movement certainly embraced a militaristic approach, but not always a supremacist approach. It was formed originally as the Black Panther Party for Self-Defense. And the self-defence was meant to be against police brutality. Where Baldwin and King criticised Black Power was when it spilled over to Black Supremacy. Baldwin thought that tragic. And it is tragic. Any supremacy leads to hierarchies of dehumanisation. In any case, and possibly because of these complexities, Baldwin not only "[felt] an undeniable tenderness towards" members of the Black Power movement, as conceded by the authors — he understood them and even conceded "intellectual grounds" to them. For example, in his letter to Angela Davis (quoted in part in *Uncivil Wars*), he acknowledged the "enormous revolution in black consciousness" occurring in the younger generation. Baldwin even appealed to Davis not to "appear to be your father's daughter in the same way that I am my father's son." Baldwin recognised that he, like his father, was constrained by what was expected of their generation and what was often sold as the model of a good black leader. He stated, with a force that is confronting, that his father "was just a n*gger — a n*gger laborer preacher, and so was I." It is remarkable how much intellectual ground Baldwin concedes to the younger generation and to this "revolution in black consciousness." Such intellectual humility is hard to come by in our era, where younger generations are often castigated as woke snowflakes who are unable to keep their calm or a job.

Above all, however, whatever his disagreement with the Black Power movement, Baldwin never made their reaction, contemptuous or otherwise, the cause of the American racial problem. He simply did not commit the error this Quarterly Essay makes by focusing not on the source of contempt, but on the victim's reaction to contempt. Baldwin in fact called out the apparent hypocrisy when he noted that "violence and heroism have been made synonymous except when it comes to blacks." He argued the only way to deal with those who embrace militant acts, like Malcom X, isn't to point to triumphs and progress made so far, but to concede that they are right and ask why this is so. Therefore, Baldwin had a radically different approach to the one proposed by Aly and Stephens. And he was right never to lose sight of the source of contempt. And here lies the greatest challenge to the authors' arguments.

Of all the "greatest advocates for racial justice" that are named in the essay, none had a fate that was drastically different from the fate of the "tragic" Black Power movement. Du Bois, a civil rights pioneer and intellectual, renounced his American citizenship and died in Ghana. Baldwin was worried "nothing has changed in the depths" and that America might be in "worse trouble than before." He spent significant time in France and died there. King was assassinated.

It is telling that King, despite a lifetime commitment to non-violence, suffered a similar fate to Black Panthers members who – as Baldwin sorrowfully lamented – were killed "like rats." So, despite the authors implying that the Black Power movement's failure was determined by its contemptuous approach, it can equally be explained by its members being killed, sometimes in their beds.

Of course, Aly and Stephens' explanation remains consistent with their claim that responding to contempt with contempt is not wise because it might attract worse outcomes. This, however, creates a circular argument. Why did the people who arrested or killed members of the Black Power movement not respond with "brotherly love" or non-contempt? After all, as Baldwin pointed out, "there is no reason that black men should be expected to be more patient, more forbearing, more farseeing than white." Is the moral responsibility for resisting contempt one that is only imposed on the contemned? And if it is only imposed on the contemned, mainly because any other reaction might result in a worse kind of contempt for the contemned, what is the point of moralising if there is only one moral possibility? And what are the practical consequences of a moral duty upheld by a threat? Isn't that analogous to the claim that a slave contract was legitimate because, as summarised by Fukuyama, "a weak individual faced [with] a choice between a life of slavery or death at the hands of a stronger person ... could voluntarily choose to be a slave"? Whatever the response to these questions, Dr King's violent assassination diminishes any claim that the manner of protest, and not what is being protested, is the problem.

Whatever the authors might believe to be the "record of lasting change" of non-contemptuous actions, Dr King's own view of that record isn't that glorious. Neither was the public's at the time. Dr King died with a disapproval rating of nearly 75 per cent – a figure that is noted by James C. Cobb as "shocking in its own day and still striking even in today's highly polarized political climate." He became beloved after his death. Reading King's own assessment of his life's work, and what was happening to it in his lifetime, is heart-breaking. In his essay "Impasse in Race Relation," Dr King spoke of white backlash and the undoing of civil rights progress. These were some of his last statements on racism, poverty and war before he was killed:

The depravity of the white backlash shattered the hopes that new attitudes were in the making. The reversion to barbaric white conduct marked by a succession of murders in the south, the recrudescent of white hoodlumism in northern cities and coldly systematic withdrawal of support by some erstwhile white allies constituted a grim statement to Negroes. They were told there were firm limits to their progress; that they must expect to remain permanently unequal and permanently poor.

According to Lawrence Glickman, writing in *The Atlantic*, white backlash has been a defining pattern of American history. For Glickman, the elements of white backlash to the civil rights movement were its smouldering resentment, its belief that the movement was proceeding "too fast," its demands for emotional and psychological sympathy, and its displacement of African Americans' struggles with its own claims of grievance. Glickman notes this backlash often deployed "imagined coercion where it did not exist" and "embraced a lexicon and posture of victimization." It was reported at the time, for example, that "white panic" was driven by fears of "favoritism" and "special privileges" for African Americans and fears that "the Negros want to take over the country." It doesn't take much to see how these fears and anxieties parallel many of the complaints of Trump supporters and the white working class that the authors write about in their essay. What is even more striking is how early in American history the charge of "favouritism" arose in response to calls for equality. Less than twenty years after the abolition of slavery, the United States Supreme Court nullified the *Civil Rights Act* of 1875 on the grounds that it was time for former enslaved people to cease "to be the special favorite of the laws."

Aly and Stephens present the matter of poor and working-class whites as something that complicates the picture, yet the picture is less complicated than it is historically consistent. Besides, the argument proceeds as if there are no poor or working-class non-whites. There are. Yet these groups don't appear to be making the same political choices or rushing into the Trump coalition. Even warning that focusing on aggregated advantages accrued by white people (like over-representation of white men in politics) should be avoided because it obscures the experiences of working-class whites, it is not long before we hit another inconsistency. It is there in the bodies that don't seem to be registered in the warning about "body-counts."

The authors challenge those who see a "democratic case for contempt" to show "its track record of lasting change." They argue that the alternative, such as when contempt underwrites decisive political action, "always involves body-counts." But there are still body-counts. The body-count has not stopped for some. Sexist contempt kills at least one Australian woman a week through domestic violence. Racist contempt killed George Floyd as he begged to breathe the air we are told is collectively ours. Placing the moral responsibility for resisting contempt on those who are contemned, on the basis that this might avoid deadly contempt against them, isn't necessarily going to prevent their deaths. We might simply fail to notice those deaths; that is, fail to include them in body-counts because they are not the kind of death that matters, or they are the kind of death we lament but tactically accept as an unavoidable price of patiently waiting for the "moral possibilities of persuasion" to return better outcomes. But since the authors remind us we should not aggregate the advantages accrued by white people to obscure the experiences of working-class whites, perhaps then we should not aggregate the progress made so far to obscure the price that continues to be paid. This reality might be tolerable if the authors' moral arguments improve the outcome. I do not think they do.

The real problem isn't necessarily the nature of contemned reaction – whether contemptuous, or Baldwinian love, or King's non-violence – it is progress itself. In short, in the case of race, white people see equality as a zero-sum game. Research confirms that "white Americans perceive increases in racial equality as threatening their dominant position in American society." This view, as noted in the section on white backlash, isn't new. It is a pattern. In the context of gender, a modern version of this zero-sum view is reflected in Scott Morrison's comment that: "We want to see women rise. But we don't want to see women rise only on the basis of others doing worse." This zero-sum frame means that what appears or feels contemptuous might be the very progress of the person – no matter how they do it. This means the contemned need not display any of the distilled characteristics of contempt for a negative reaction to occur. I do not know how we resolve that, but perhaps, like Baldwin, we can better witness to our times.

Baldwin considered himself foremost a witness. We read him today and get a clear picture of what was the sin, who were the sinners, what price was paid, and how we might possibly liberate ourselves, or indeed perish. The task of a witness is to record things as they saw them. What, then, does *Uncivil Wars* stand as a witness to? Is it an accurate assessment of our time? What, as a matter of style and approach, does it "insist on"? How does it focus "our attention" on some things while "narrowing our attention on others"? Could we really say that cancel culture and political correctness create as symmetrical a threat to democracy as the concerted efforts by Republicans to restrict voting rights in a way that recalls America at the time of Reconstruction?

Wherever our future lies, whether in the grace of equality or in the doom of body-counts, it is not for the contemned to be blamed. Those to be blamed are the ones who insist on that type of innocence Baldwin called criminal. They seek to hold others in perpetual contempt, and human dignity refuses to be divisible. There is little that is theoretically appealing about obtaining one dignity partially or gradually through the "hard labour of patient appeal." That this has been practically the case is a kind of moral failure which has had deadly consequences. The chance for change lies in challenging that moral failure, not in elevating it as the appropriate form of relating to one another. Even if the contemned have to reconcile themselves with a harsh reality in order to survive, it is never morally wrong not to lose sight of the whole claim to dignity and to insist that it become reality. That it is reality unjustly withheld.

Nyadol Nyuon

Carla Wilshire

What is most exceptional about *Uncivil Wars* is not what it covers, but what it leaves out. In a treatise on the fragility and risks of American democracy, it is telling that the 6 January riots are not mentioned. Neither are declining institutional trust, voter suppression, gerrymandering, Russian interference or disinformation. A definition essay by design, it industriously explores the topology and nuance of a singular impassioned hypothesis – contempt. This fervent state, we are told, has metastasised in the milieu of algorithmic social media and is now eating away our political institutions from within, consuming the very skeleton of our democracy. The proposed remedy is less "cancel culture" and more courtesy, lest we engender civil war.

The essay presents a three-tiered model of contempt, defined by an escalating moral dimension. The third form of contempt, implicitly the most malicious, is moral censure, where an individual or group is judged by their behaviour to have an irredeemable failing of character. The example given is online "cancel culture," where subjects are targeted and judged for transgressing a moral standard held by a contemptuous group. This third form of contempt, described as a deliberate and considered act of moral appraisal culminating in a "totalising" and unrecoverable verdict of inferior human worth, is characterised as bidirectional, but in practice no examples of upward contempt are given (women morally censuring men, black people censuring white).

I take issue with their deeply flawed construction on three grounds. Firstly, it ignores the contested (and sometimes violent) history of social progress in favour of a nostalgic view of democracy as a polite "to-and-fro" of ideas. Secondly, while American democracy is at a critical juncture, increased contempt is a symptom and not a cause. Contempt is an emotive state born of a process – in this case polarisation – rather than a causal factor. Contributing factors include increasing economic inequality, disinformation and the rise of the authoritarian right. Finally, the role of social media needs to be considered more fully. In an unregulated public square, many of the examples of online contempt should be examined through the lens not of individual human emotion, but of group dynamics. There is an issue with the categorisation of cancel culture as contempt; it is instead a sometimes brutal, sometimes justified form of group social regulation.

Gloria Steinem once said that, "Power can be taken, but not given. The process of the taking is empowerment in itself." Cultural and political change is rarely won quietly or politely and never without contest. American democracy is an act of creation that spans centuries, its ledger defined by more periods of division than unity and more accounts of contest than accord. At its inception, the constitution did not deliver for most Americans. The frontiers of American democracy, its basic structures of government, voter rights and the role of courts have always been fiercely debated, but the system has enjoyed a level of institutional continuity through world wars, terrorist attacks, the civil rights movement, women's liberation, the Vietnam War. It is striking that in an essay portraying democracy as a casualty of the uncivil disobedience of online cancel culture, there is a conspicuous omission of the essential threads of contestation that weave strength into the fabric of America's democracy.

The ultimate endgame of mutual contempt, Aly and Stephens argue, is the inability to engage in civil debate and the hardening of ideological positions. This presumably undermines the building blocks of democracy for two reasons; firstly, democracy requires an exchange of ideas that contempt does not allow for; and secondly, contempt undermines the collective narrative that is necessary for the functioning of a democratic state. I do not disagree with these general claims. We are in a period of heightened polarisation, and one of the indications of this is indeed contempt. However, contempt itself is not what is causing American democracy to falter. Contempt is a limited individual human emotion, while polarisation is a complex multifaceted process that can be created by myriad factors.

Firstly, polarisation is a manifestation of economic inequality. To put this in more concrete terms, the richest 10 per cent of US households own 70 per cent of total wealth (with half held by the top 1 per cent), and the bottom 50 per cent hold only 5 per cent of total wealth. Furthermore, Thomas Piketty finds that while in the 1970s the cumulative value of inherited wealth constituted only around half of total wealth, by 2030 this figure will be between 80 and 90 per cent.

This point is central. A polity that does not enable upward economic mobility and does not reward merit will create an increasingly disenfranchised and angry citizenry. The patterns of history show that although democracies can survive internal conflict, they tend to fare poorly in the absence of economic mobility. We need to believe we can succeed.

Secondly, while Aly and Stephens accurately identify both sensational tabloids and social media as a risk to modern democracy through the distribution of disinformation and "fake news," their exploration is limited to the role each medium plays in creating a more contemptuous polity.

Disinformation is a strategy employed by a growing number of state and non-state actors, including those on the far right. It is a low-cost, high-yield means to spread narratives, distort opinion and undermine trust in public institutions. As Christina Nemr and William Gangware write in their report "Weapons of Mass Destruction," disinformation campaigns often work to simplify complex problems and can be framed to provide consumers of content with a belief that they are exposing hidden truths. An example of a disinformation campaign in this vein is QAnon. In *The Wall Street Journal*, Brett Forrest explains how QAnon offers a definitive explanation to combat uncertainty and to explain complex global outcomes. It has also undermined trust in American democracy and the institutions of government.

Social media can be utilised to destabilise, erode trust, confuse messaging or flood public opinion. This does make people more angry and thus more contemptuous, but more importantly it erodes their belief in democracy. Some 80 per cent of Republicans consider the 2020 election to have been stolen, and this belief was sown by an organised campaign of disinformation led by Donald Trump. The 6 January riot was the single most fractious day in American democracy during our lifetimes. It is a testament to the leaning of Aly and Stephens' essay that it is not mentioned once. A result of social media disinformation might be contempt, but the cause is deliberate and orchestrated campaigns to sow the seeds of mistruth and mistrust.

It was Trump's contempt for democratic institutions and the operating rules of elections that fuelled the 6 January protesters. The MAGA right − Trump's Republican apparatus − won the 2016 election by appealing to the section of America who had the least experience in American democratic traditions, and so the least attachment to democracy. As Yoni Appelbaum writes in *The Atlantic*: "In 2016, a presidential candidate who scorned established norms rode that contempt to the Republican nomination, drawing his core support from Americans who seldom participate in the rituals of democracy."

It is this "fourth" form of contempt − not towards people, but towards the very values that underpin their own political system − that represents the biggest threat to American democracy in 2024.

Finally, the authors misunderstand that group censure is part of social regulation. Democracies enshrine collective values in the law and enforce them in the courts. Social media is our new public square and, as a privately regulated sphere, it relies on group moderation, which can be swift and sharp, and on reporting to the platform when agreed values are contravened. At the extremes, internet censure involves de-platforming, a kind of internet prison if you will. How and when this should be used is worthy of debate. But is this contempt? Contempt is an individual emotion. "Cancel culture" as defined by the authors is not; it is a form of social regulation, perhaps sometimes unwarranted or even toxic, perhaps sometimes necessary. It is worth noting that there is no collectively agreed definition of cancel culture. The term itself was popularised by the American right and cyber-libertarians. That said, survey data collected by the Pew Research Center shows that the most accepted definition across both conservative Republicans and liberal Democrats is "actions people take to hold others accountable." The same research indicates that the majority of Americans support the calling out of others on social media for potentially offensive content. "Cancel culture" is not necessarily "trolling" or a "pile-on"; sometimes it is simply the act of drawing moral boundaries and pushing back on the contempt of others, and sometimes it is just evidence of shifting cultural norms.

I arrived at the end of the essay unnerved that it makes only a passing mention of poverty, fake news and echo chambers, and then only as examples of contempt and not as drivers of polarisation. The true risks to democracy – the rise of the far right and the seeping of authoritarian doctrine into Republican ideology and practice – are conveniently ignored. The writers attempt to shoehorn the reader into a view that democracy is at risk, not from authoritarianism, but from cancel culture and the growth of an uncivil polity. Perhaps the most damning irony is that Aly and Stephens themselves censure those who, after years in sufferance of "downward contempt" from those who stand above them in the established social order, are now exercising power "upward."

When they reach their conclusion, Aly and Stephens offer no remedies beyond polite conversation. But there are many. The solutions lie in a progressive government that embraces taxation on wealth, equitable education, universal healthcare and welfare as countervailing measures to the tendencies of unfettered markets, and in the regulation of social media and a broad-based investment in critical media skills. They are found in projects that rebuild trust in institutions and in narratives of collective worth. Taxation, redistribution and education are fundamental to a thriving economy, but even more fundamental to an enduring democracy.

Carla Wilshire

John Quiggin

Uncivil *Wars* arrived in my email at the same time as two other pieces of news. The first related to the removal of a mural painted by a Melbourne artist, showing a Russian and a Ukrainian soldier embracing. It was not well received by Ukrainians, who have suffered months of murder, rape and other crimes at the hands of Russian soldiers, and would have suffered more, were it not for the fierce resistance put up by Ukraine's own forces. While this particular mural was (let us hope) an expression of a sincere wish for peace, it echoed the message of Russian propagandists (notably including Fox News contributors such as Tucker Carlson) seeking to portray the two sides as morally equivalent.

Contempt for Putin and his murderous supporters is entirely justified. But a natural reading of the Stephens and Aly discussion of US politics is that such contempt should stop at the water's edge, exempting people like Carlson because of "the bond that must exist between democratic citizens." Certainly, that's the implication of their view that Hillary Clinton's description of millions of Trump supporters as racists was outrageous contempt, even though there is ample evidence that it was accurate.

More directly relevant to the essay was President Biden's speech on 1 September warning that US democracy was under threat from MAGA extremists. Republicans responded to the speech with attack lines that might have been drawn directly from the Stephens and Aly essay. Biden, Republicans said, was slandering tens of millions of Americans as "fascists." In Australia, a string of pieces in the Murdoch press echoed this view.

But what led Biden to make such statements? It is hard to think of an American politician more steeped in the old-fashioned ways of consensus, learned from decades in the Senate. His election campaign was premised, in large measure, on his ability to work "across the aisle" with Republicans. And even in his doom-laden speech, Biden was careful to claim that such Republicans still exist.

Has Biden suddenly fallen, as the analysis of Stephens and Aly would seem to imply, into a politics of grievance and contempt? Or was he, perhaps, responding to a series of events they don't even mention (with the exception of a passing reference to the quite literal call to "hang Mike Pence")? Somehow, the repeated attempts by Republicans to overthrow US democracy, of which the most dramatic was the 6 January insurrection, seem to have escaped their notice.

The desperate attempts at moral equivalence in this essay can be seen not only on big points like this, but also in more trivial pieces of bias. Stephens and Aly quote, with approval, a report in *Vox* on the social psychology of threats. This reflects the fact that *Vox* is a serious publication, offering careful analysis from a broadly progressive, but not propagandistic, perspective. Yet when they want to denounce "tabloid" partisan media, Stephens and Aly list "Fox, *Vox*, Sky, *Vice*, *BuzzFeed* and the *Daily Mail*," carefully balancing right-wing propaganda outlets with titles that might be seen as leftish.

At a time when democracy is under threat around the world, the last thing we need is right-wing advocacy packaged as "both sides do it" centrism. But that is precisely what Stephens and Aly have offered us.

John Quiggin

Brigid Delaney

Recently, the *New York Times* podcast *The Daily* reported on the story of a pastor in Arkansas. Kevin Thompson, forty-four, was solidly Republican, a small "c" conservative who had happily and without much complaint led his congregation in his hometown of Fort Smith for nineteen years. As he tended to the community, his flock grew and things were going well. Thompson thought he'd be there for life. Until 2016. Trump was running for president — and some aspects of his character did not jibe with Thompson's moral code.

Thompson wrote a blog post that said that for the first time in his life, he would not be voting Republican that election. Instead, he would seek out an independent candidate.

All hell broke loose inside the parish. The upshot was that the parishioners did not want to be challenged on their political beliefs. They did not want to hear another side or another point of view. After a couple of other clashes around political and cultural issues, it became apparent that Thompson had lost the authority to preach. He and his family left Arkansas and moved to California.

"The moment you lose the concept of truth you've lost everything," he told *The Daily*. And he might have also said, "The moment we lose the ability to disagree, we've lost everything." As the great Roman Stoic Seneca wrote almost two thousand years ago: "We are bad men living among bad men; and only one thing can calm us — we must agree to go easy on one another."

What happened to the Arkansas pastor was a failure on one side to agree to disagree. As a consequence, he was cancelled for the crime of misspeaking.

We often think cancellation is a bloodless attack that occurs online and then people move onto a new victim (or main character, as it's known in Twitter parlance) the next day. But people are being cancelled in real life all the time — not just for expressing views that are offensive or defamatory, but also for ideas that differ from the orthodoxy of the community hearing them.

Thompson's views were pretty benign. He wrote that he intended to vote independent. But in a society that is rife with inflammation and division (caused in part by misinformation and fake news), even a mild divergence from the norm is enough to find one cast off into the outer darkness.

It used to be that living harmoniously in a community or small town meant living with a variety of views and positions, some that may be different from your own. The old taboo on talking about religion, politics or money, once seen as outdated and quaint, now appears to have played an important social role. It kept us all from tearing each other apart.

Communities are more cohesive and less fractured – and also more diverse – when there are fewer arguments about religious, cultural and political positions.

But living in smaller communities, made up of a range of people with differing beliefs, also acts to stretch our limits of tolerance. And this can only be a good thing. If your neighbour votes differently from you, but you rely on your neighbour to help you in the garden or lend you tools or drop your kids at school, you are less likely to cut him off for his political beliefs. Now, with social media, the internet allows you to form your own communities around beliefs, political positions, sexual and cultural identities and religion. In many ways it is the opposite of lived communities, where you have to take what you get in terms of neighbours and other community members. Internet communities strengthen and reinforce bonds by virtue of their common beliefs. With this strengthened group identity, we go out into the world and – as Waleed Aly and Scott Stephens explore in their essay – we feel more empowered not only to assert our own beliefs but also to reject the beliefs of those who may disagree or have other opinions.

So, what to do about this? We can't rewind the internet, but we can balance it – and our online communities – with engagement in the real world. It's harder to condemn and castigate someone to their face (although, in the case of Pastor Thompson, it's getting easier in lived communities as well).

And remember this: "Only one thing can calm us – we must agree to go easy on one another."

Brigid Delaney

Martin Krygier

I welcome and applaud Waleed Aly and Scott Stephens' trenchant critique of the growth of contempt as a standard accompaniment (and source) of hostilities among citizens "in public settings." They argue elegantly and rightly that, as a reflex response to those with whom we differ, contempt pollutes "the quality of the air we breathe together," and corrodes democracy, civil society and indeed most other conditions that might sustain successful and flourishing lives in common.

Of course, as so many contemnors happily learn, a posture of reflexive contempt for those with whom one disagrees has its charms. It allows the alluring pleasures of self-righteous and censorious judgment, demands neither excuse nor apology, does wonders for one's confidence, and allows one to avoid the difficult business of mounting or coping with evidence and argument. But these are shabby delights, typically unearned by those who enjoy them and undeserved by those who suffer from them.

But what's the alternative? The essay's title is "uncivil wars," but clearly Aly and Stephens are not after civil wars, a phrase in which the adjective has another "other." A civil war is, of course, not a war that is civil, but a war among citizens. The opposite of uncivil wars is civil peace, not a common phrase but an attractive condition for which we have a more familiar term: civil society.

Often, when civil society is spoken of today, the adjective has little work to do. The noun carries the whole load. It's a way of turning attention to society rather than, say, the state or government or even the economy. Alternatively, and today typically, civil society is degraded simply to identify a particular sub-category of organisations within society at large: NGOs, or "not-for-profits." This might be what led to the lament by the Hungarian former anti-communist dissident Ferenc Miszlivetz that "what we dreamed of was civil society. What we got were NGOs." One senses he hoped for more.

What did they dream of? Perhaps a society in which routine relations among citizens are not dominated by the state and are actually, and typically, expected to be routinely civil, rather than hostile, warlike, full of mutual contempt and/or worse. For a special charm of societies in which civility is widespread, as I argued in my essay "The Quality of Civility," is that:

> routine non-predatory social relations can occur among non-intimates that neither depend upon love or deep connection nor – as is common in uncivil conditions – are fractured by their absence and replaced by suspicion, hostility, hatred, or simple fear. Cool, civil connections are not the only ones that occur nor should they be, but in the public realm the possibility of such connections is key. People have familial, ethnic, religious, and linguistic attachments that often matter to them greatly and that differ; but they do not kill for them. Nor is it a realistic expectation that they might.

Civility in this sense is cooler than love – if all you can say of lovers is that they behave civilly to each other, you know the relationship is on the rocks. In its place, however, civility is precious, for it is cooler and calmer than hatred as well. It doesn't just happen though, but is a true and relatively rare achievement. As we know from many parts of the world, it doesn't have to be like that. In so many places, today and always, society is not composed of routinely civil exchanges and interchanges among citizens but of wary and hostile manoeuvres, full of tension, fear, hatred and, often, contempt.

Many of the societies with which Aly and Stephens are concerned, with all their myriad faults, blemishes and real sins – including our own – have attained a high level of civility (at least among large numbers of their citizens) for considerable periods of time. That depended on a host of enabling conditions, which are often in short supply and, as we are seeing in the United States and many countries, can dry up or be deliberately destroyed. Manufacture and distribution of wholesale contempt, as Aly and Stephens show, threaten this precious condition and achievement.

I doubt that they would disagree with any of this. However, they never mention civil society, and they seem to have something altogether different and more demanding in mind as the ideal antidote to contempt, which we should strive to emulate, if not completely realise. The model is marriage. Thus their first example of contempt arises in the context of a marriage gone wrong. There, a wife who believes her husband is prepared to use her as sexual traffic for a job (for that is what it amounts to) finds him contemptible (as, were the charge justified, would I). And their last chapter, entitled "Democracy as Marriage," makes clear that the ideal to emulate as a counter to contempt is a marriage gone right: "a particular type of relationship in which two persons, who are bound together by nothing more substantial than a reciprocal devotion, discover through their life together the 'ethical conditions' that allow their union to persist."

I'm fond of democracy, I like many of my neighbours, some of them are friends and some of them I love. I'm also fond of marriage. But to hope for much like "a reciprocal devotion" among citizens of vast, multitudinous, various, differentiated society – who, unlike many spouses, have no opportunity to choose (or to leave) their associates – seems to aim a little high. It is what philosophers used to call a category mistake.

Just as modernity was taking shape, Adam Smith wonderfully characterised the predicament of the citizen of modern, large, populous, complex, differentiated societies: "In civilised societies, he [sic] stands at all times in need of the co-operation and assistance of great multitudes, while his whole life is scarce sufficient to gain the friendship of a few persons." If he or she is lucky, one of those persons might be a spouse and their relationship "nothing more substantial than a reciprocal devotion." But that's a rather fragile foundation on which to build a society among multitudes, the bulk of whose social relationships must necessarily be unchosen and thin, unlike those of spouses, whose connections, for better or worse, richer or poorer, are thick.

To be helpful, an ideal for social interaction must take seriously the circumstances of politics and society, as they are and as they are likely to be. Sustaining conditions of civility does that; seeking society-wide simulations of reciprocal devotion does not. There are two routes to this conclusion, one born of relative but realistic optimism, the other of bleak pessimism, about the human condition. Both need to be taken seriously.

On the one hand, whereas civility is often regarded as a cold and pallid virtue, the optimistic civilian stresses how much it can offer to social interaction that is rich and positive. This view is nowhere expressed with more insight and nuance than in a chapter (on civility and piety) of *The Moral Commonwealth*, the magnum opus of the great American sociologist Philip Selznick.

Selznick was that very rare type of thinker, a Hobbesian idealist. Unlike most people, who tend to emphasise either conditions of survival (Hobbes) or hopes for flourishing (ideals), he insisted that we should strive to realise both: recognise real constraints, but refuse to ignore ideal potential, which he tried very hard to find. But conditions precede possibilities: without survival, flourishing is not an option. On the one hand, he writes, civility is "not a morality of engagement . . .

It is cool, not hot, detached, not involved" and it is a necessary condition for secure interactions among those who will never love each other. It is true, as Selznick was at pains to stress, that more might be possible. Indeed, where circumstances are favourable, the qualities of civility might be enriched, for:

> Respect is not love, but it strains toward love as it gains substance and subtlety. Rudimentary respect is formal, external, and rule-centered − founded in fear of disruption and lack of cooperation. The corresponding civility can be chilly indeed, as some connotations of "being civil" suggest. An important change occurs when respect is informed by genuine appreciation for the values at stake in communication and good order ...
>
> In truly civil communication, for example, something more is required than self-restraint and taking turns. An effort must be made really to listen, that is, to understand and appreciate what someone else is saying. As we do so we move from arm's-length "inter-action" to more engaged "interaction." We discover and create shared meanings; the content or substance of the discussion becomes more important than the form. The outcome is often a particular community of discourse and a unique social bond. A foundation is laid for affection and commitment ...
>
> Furthermore, civil speech takes into account human frailties and sensibilities. Contempt is the enemy of communication; patience and empathy are its allies. Hence we reject as uncivil personal abuse, intellectual intimidation, and indifference to offense. On especially sensitive issues − religion, nationality, race, for example − civil communication treads lightly, with special regard for the sources of personal identity.

In these passages, Selznick comes closer than elsewhere to countenancing the ideals that Aly and Stephens espouse, though they are ideals for enriched public, not intimate, engagement. And that is never where he *starts*. For while he always hoped for more, he realised that often circumstances don't give you much choice. You might aim for high ceilings, but you must start with solid foundations. It is harder the other way round.

Our world is full of dark possibilities, repeatedly realised. Even then, indeed especially then, where love is nowhere to be found and we confront just how perilous the circumstances of society and politics can be, norms and practices of cool civility among associates and strangers are precious.

This darker, more uniformly Hobbesian theme has recently been taken up by the Oxford political theorist Teresa Bejan in her book *Mere Civility*. Writing of the seventeenth-century debates over the novel idea of toleration, she introduces us – well, she introduced me – to one Roger Williams, a now somewhat obscure but then significant English Puritan evangelist and religious fanatic, who founded and became governor of the colony of Rhode Island in America. He advocated the practice of "meer [sic] civility" as the "*vinculum societatis*" (social bond) that, as Bejan puts it, "might hold in the face of protracted fundamental disagreement and discord" that followed the Protestant Reformation. On this view, "the virtue of civility in a tolerant society rested on the way in which the rules of respectful behaviour could be maintained no matter what one thought about others, their culture or their fundamental and sacred beliefs." The blunt message was, "[w]hile we are stuck in the same boat with people we hate, we better make the most of it."

Williams has been taken up recently by those few political theorists who have heard of him, prominent among them Martha Nussbaum, as an inspiring prophet of civility as a product and source of mutual respect, if not love. However, on Bejan's persuasive reinterpretation he was nothing of the kind. It was lack of respect for beliefs other than his own that drove him and that he sought to deal with. This Puritan zealot appeared to dislike, to the point of disgust, the views of anyone who did not share his beliefs, and in Rhode Island, as well as in England, there were a lot of them. He expected he would not be alone in that sentiment. So rather than decree the impossible, that we should respect the views of those with whom we disagreed over the most fundamental things, he made available in Rhode Island, and enforced, an extraordinary and unprecedented freedom of religious belief, speech and observance.

Bejan argues that Williams had recognised a truth for which there is more than enough evidence and good reason to believe: that many of the harshest problems of social life, perhaps inexorable problems, come simply from the difficulties people have in living peacefully with others whose views, or whose religion, or whose nationality, or whose ethnicity, colour, gender ... they do not share. Of course, we can be directed to like and respect them, but often that doesn't work. What to do? Williams' answer was not to try to wish fundamental disagreements away, but to acknowledge they were here to stay and we had to have ways of dealing peaceably with them. His answer, translated by Bejan to the modern world, might seem dispiriting from a marriage guidance counsellor, yet apt for a social analyst. He faced then, and we face now, the problem that very often:

> [in] trying to make sense of others' different opinions, human
> beings conclude not that these differences are reasonable by-products

of the burdens of judgment but that their opponents are bigoted, ignorant, malicious, even insane. We might hope – and strive – to do otherwise. But rather than conflating this aspiration with civility, political theorists [and the rest of us] must recognize the latter as the virtue called upon to fill the breach when reality fails to meet our expectations.

In such circumstances, exhortations to treat others as we should a loved partner, instead,

> necessarily move the discussion to an *aspirational* realm of ideal theory in which the kinds of problems civility is needed to address *do not even arise*. The result is an impoverishment of our ethical vocabulary, which, in turn, exacerbates the vacuity of our moral and political discourse in confronting the very problems to which we appeal to civility and toleration as solutions.

Bejan is here talking us down from expectations that "mutual respect," still less John Locke's "love and charity in the diversity of contrary opinions," can be relied on to serve as lubricants for harmonious and civil social relations. Doubtless, they are good things to have, but one wouldn't bet on them. One might nevertheless hope that Selznick's realistic optimism will be vindicated in some societies at some times, but we know that bleaker options are more likely in much of the world. One wonders, in either circumstance, what the odds are for sustaining modern societies on "nothing more substantial than a reciprocal devotion."

Martin Krygier

Robert B. Talisse

There is much to admire in Waleed Aly and Scott Stephens' essay. Its strength lies in the care with which Aly and Stephens analyse their central diagnostic concept, *contempt*. Their claim is that although current democratic politics admits of many forms of dysfunction, the root problem is neither disunity nor animosity, nor polarisation, but rather the fact that these forces are driven by the disposition of contempt. On their view, contempt is the tendency to treat all political disagreement as an existential conflict between democracy and tyranny, and the corresponding disposition to write off anyone with whom one disagrees as wholly beyond the pale and thus undeserving of engagement.

As Aly and Stephens observe, when contempt takes hold of our civic life, our political divides grow to be at once both deep and shallow. We're convinced that fundamental democratic norms are at stake in every dispute. Yet those disputes are increasingly grounded in self-serving caricatures of the opposing side. Politics becomes intensely disagreeable, but increasingly detached from any actual disagreement.

I find Aly and Stephens' essay largely correct. However, I also think their account is incomplete. In this brief response, I will introduce an additional element into their diagnostic story. In turn, this addition will complicate Aly and Stephens' analysis of what we must do to restore democracy.

Something's amiss, isn't it? Definitely. It is common among democratic theorists and practitioners to begin from the assumption that democratic dysfunctions emerge always from the ways in which citizens, officials and institutions fall short of democracy's demands. We can call this assumption the Addams–Dewey Principle, as it is captured in the slogan that Jane Addams and John Dewey popularised: "the cure for democracy's ills is more democracy." Here "more democracy" means "better democracy"; hence the idea is that all democratic dysfunctions are at root democratic failings. In this way, the

Addams–Dewey Principle forms the basis for another fundamental commitment of Dewey's conception of democracy: democratic ends can be achieved only through democratic means.

The Addams–Dewey Principle is undeniably attractive. Indeed, a broad range of political dysfunctions can be traced to our institutions, practices and habits being insufficiently democratic. Yet the principle is too often read as universal in scope, as saying that *whatever the dysfunction may be, the solution is more democracy.* The Addams–Dewey Principle thus denies that there could be a form of democratic dysfunction that arises precisely because citizens are earnestly attempting to satisfy their civic duties.

The Addams–Dewey Principle is false. As I argued in my 2019 book, *Overdoing Democracy*, certain civic virtues can be cultivated only under conditions where citizens occasionally engage in cooperative social activities in which politics has no place. One upshot of this argument is that the tendency to see in every activity a potential site of democratic participation is actually counter-productive. In overdoing democracy in this way, we undermine it – we erode the civic virtues we need to perform well as citizens. Overdone democracy is itself a kind of democratic dysfunction. More democracy thus can lead to worse democracy. It seems to me that Aly and Stephens have tacitly embraced the Addams–Dewey Principle, or at least not attended to the ways in which political contempt may itself be a predictable product of authentic democratic engagement.

In my 2021 book, *Sustaining Democracy*, I argued that democratic citizenship is intrinsically morally conflicted. On the one hand, citizens are obligated to deploy their share of political power to advance justice as they can best discern it. That is, democratic citizens must take *responsibility for* their politics by participating, individually and collectively, in the project of making a more just political order. On the other hand, citizens are also required to recognise the political equality of their fellow citizens. They are *responsible to* others, including those among the citizenry with whom they disagree over justice. They must regard their fellow citizens as people who not only *get* an equal political say, but *are entitled* to one. On many accounts of democracy, citizens are additionally required to *consider* and perhaps *consult* their fellow citizens when deciding how to best pursue justice.

The conflict between these two modes of democratic responsibility is manifest. Especially when political issues are urgent, the obligation to pursue justice can run counter to the obligation to recognise our fellow citizens as our equals. After all, to adopt a position about what justice requires is to see opposing positions as not merely mistaken, but *in the wrong.* We hence are bound to see our political opponents as not merely on the *wrong* side of the issues, but on the *unjust* side. The requirement to be responsible to our foes thus seems to encumber our effort to pursue justice. A democratic citizen might well wonder why she should extend to her opponents any consideration whatsoever, given that they are on the side of injustice. In *Sustaining Democracy*, I call this conflict the "democrat's dilemma." It's important to observe that it arises out of a sincere commitment to the ethics of democratic citizenship rather than to some dereliction.

Consider a further upshot of the dilemma. In order to have an effective voice in a democracy, one needs to join a chorus. Accordingly, the project of taking responsibility for our politics necessarily involves building coalitions of like-minded others. As members of coalitions, we must plan and coordinate joint endeavours, and we thus grow to rely on other members to support and advocate for the collective. In any modern democracy, the dynamics of democratic social activism are shaky. To succeed, the movement must be sustained, and this calls for high levels of sustained commitment and effort among large numbers of individuals. Solidarity, integrity, cooperation and persistence are crucial; correspondingly, it is important for coalitions to weed out any poseurs or pretenders in their ranks. This means that activist coalitions tend to establish, formally or informally, litmus tests for authenticity among the members, ways of assuring the other members that one is "all in" with the group's cause and agenda.

Here the democrat's dilemma intensifies. Showing political opponents due regard, "attending" to them in the ways that Aly and Stephens recommend, typically appears to one's allies as a signal of inauthenticity or half-heartedness. Why seek to give the other side a hearing, unless one thinks they may have something of value to say? To see the opposition as anything other than an obstacle to justice, to see them as deserving of "attention," is to *concede* something to injustice. Thus, in charged contexts of political engagement, the attempt to make good on the responsibility to our fellow citizens can jeopardise our political coalitions, thereby undermining our efforts to promote justice.

This point about the need for in-group solidarity is important because, in line with the Addams–Dewey Principle, Aly and Stephens seem to place the cause of contempt entirely within the commodified and commercial informational environments that democratic citizens now inhabit. Their diagnosis here is correct as far as it goes. The problem is that it doesn't go far enough. My suggestion is that escalating partisan contempt and the corresponding tendency to write off anyone who's not an overt political ally is incentivised by the very nature of democratic social action. Citizens cultivate and express contempt as a way of signalling authenticity to their political allies, and in doing this they assure them of their allyship. Although such measures are democratically dysfunctional, they are nonetheless necessary for building and sustaining viable political coalitions. Once again, the dysfunction is partly due to a non-negotiable element of democracy rather than to a deviation from it.

What can be done? Aly and Stephens propose a compelling vision of healthy democracy where citizens learn to attend to one another and care for the common atmosphere of democratic "air." I embrace this view of what a healthy democracy would look like. However, in shifting from diagnostic to prescriptive analysis, it is imperative not to conflate two distinct questions: (1) how would things look were present dysfunctions mitigated? and (2) what can be done to mitigate present dysfunctions? Too often, theorists answer the second question strictly by way of the first. That is, they propose to mitigate democratic dysfunctions by asking people to act as if the dysfunctions never took hold in the first place. This is to conflate prevention and remedy.

Properly formulated, the prescriptive question is what we can do *given that* contempt is already at the core of our democracy. It seems to me that Aly and Stephens' prescription is doomed. Given that we are already in the grip of a politics rooted in partisan contempt, taking up their call for attending to our opponents is bound to dissolve our political alliances, thereby turning our political friends into additional enemies. Though I cannot here provide my alternative prescription, I believe the way forward lies not with endeavours to repair toxic relations among political foes, but rather with the attempt to expand our sense of permissible disagreement among our friends, to see authentic allyship as possible despite ongoing political disagreement. Again, given existing levels of contempt and corresponding degrees of in-group conformity, it is not clear how this can be achieved. My hunch, which is currently being worked out in a forthcoming book, is that we can begin to mitigate present dysfunctions only by reclaiming detached and solitary reflection as an essential activity of the democratic citizen.

Robert B. Talisse

Karen Jones

Emotions infuse our interactions with one another and shape our social and political worlds. The affective climate we inhabit changes our perception of the practical options that we face and of the people with whom we communicate. Many commentators claim that there has been a change in this climate and not for the better: fear, distrust, disdain and anger are on the rise, and they are driving out cooperation, trust, respect and civility. We inhabit an increasingly polarised and toxic social and political landscape. By bringing contempt into focus, Waleed Aly and Scott Stephens have taken us a step further towards understanding this present climate and, with that, a step further towards remedying it. Whereas many place current problems at anger's doorstep, Aly and Stephens diagnose contempt as the chief culprit. I will argue that, though they are not wrong to lay blame on a rush to hold those we disagree with in contempt, the philosophers they draw on misunderstand the nature of contempt. This misunderstanding leads us to find symmetry between the contempt which we might appropriately feel towards views that are beyond the pale, such as white supremacy, and the "reverse" contempt that those charged with being contemptable might direct back at us. Contempt is dangerous – even, I will argue, more dangerous than Aly and Stephens claim – but it is seldom best understood as a symmetrical problem.

Contempt has few supporters, but two philosophers, Michelle Mason and Macalester Bell, have recently taken up the job of defending it. Their analyses are similar. Both point to the totalising nature of contempt: it ascribes "badbeing" to the one held in contempt. It is not simply that the contemptible have done bad things or displayed morally problematic character traits – traits they should be ashamed of but which they might yet work to remedy. Contempt is a move to global shaming: the person's whole character, their very identity, is found wanting. The contemptible are beyond redemption. Contempt, on this analysis, passes a form of harsh moral judgment on the one held in contempt and in so doing positions the contemptuous as morally superior to their target. Contempt seeks expression in words or deeds and so is communicative. Aly and Stephens accept this analysis but reject Mason's and Bell's limited defence of the emotion, on the grounds that the evidential requirements they place on justified contempt are simply not able to be met in the public domain, given the commodification of outrage in our current environment.

I don't think this is the right analysis of contempt. This becomes clear when we consider contempt towards institutions. When Scott Morrison secretly assumed several ministerial portfolios, he demonstrated contempt towards the Westminster parliamentary system, towards his cabinet colleagues, and towards the Australian public. Yet he did not pass harsh moral judgment on the institution of Westminster parliament, his colleagues or the public. He did not ascribe "bad-being" to anyone. (It barely makes sense to say we can ascribe badbeing to institutions, though we can find them corrupt.) Morison demonstrated an unwill-ingness to be held answerable to that system, his colleagues or the public. This suggests that the core of contempt lies in the thought, "I am not answerable to you." One reason we might take this position is if we hold others to be so mor-ally bankrupt that they are outside our moral community and can therefore be pre-emptively dismissed, ignored or shunned. But it is not the only reason. We can also consider ourselves not to be answerable because of our own superiority (patronising contempt, as defined by Aly and Stephens). Neither seems easy to justify, raising the question of whether it is ever reasonable to take ourselves not to be answerable to an institution, a view, a person or a group of people. Isn't the practice of giving reasons for what we do and being responsive to the demands of others to justify our actions both at the heart of moral life and cen-tral to any well-functioning democracy? If contempt is a refusal of answerability, how could it ever be justified?

I think it can be. I think white supremacy and white supremacists are contempt-ible. In response to the violent protests in Charlottesville in 2017, Trump was just wrong to say, "you also had people that were very fine people on both sides." In our public discourse we do not have to give space to, engage with or debate white supremacy; we are done with answerability towards such views and towards such people, because they've "asked" and been "answered." Asked and answered again and again over at least the last 200 years. Answerability has been discharged.

There's dangerous territory here. What happens when one group thinks "asked and answered" and places a position and its advocates outside the sphere of answerability and open to dismissal, while another group thinks "not answered, still trying to ask, and being unfairly and contemptuously closed down"? Perhaps this characterises where the Australian community is currently at with the issue of trans inclusion. Trans activists have taken on the burden of sharing their lived experience, and of myth-busting "mad or bad" stereotypes and so might justly feel "asked and answered," yet they continue to be met with "not answered." How do we decide when the burden of answerability has been discharged and contempt becomes warranted?

There's further reason to be cautious in our contempt. Emotions have their own kind of logic. It's not the logic of argument, but a narrative logic in which some feelings invite or repel others, which in turn invite or repel yet others, which in turn ... and so on through feedback loops that can quickly turn toxic. Aly and Stephens criticise online shaming, in which someone is called out for their bad behaviour and faces the threat of being "cancelled." It is a practice of contempt, they claim. Because I have a different analysis of contempt, I don't take these practices to be expressive of contempt – yet. But there is an affective alchemy whereby they fast turn into not just contempt, but runaway contempt. If I try to shame you, I am presupposing that we share some moral standard to which we are both accountable. I charge you with failing to meet that moral standard and so showing some deficiency in your character. It is time you pulled your socks up and tried to become a better person. Sometimes this works. But more often it doesn't. Shame is a strongly negatively valenced emotion and we are strongly motivated to avoid it. Shaming is more likely to attract anger than reform. However, anger only partly meets the sting of would-be shaming. Contempt does a much better job, because it dismisses the charge at its root: I am not answerable to you, and so I am not answerable to your shaming move. I dismiss it and you, so there! You dismiss me? Well, then, I dismiss you! (Developmentally, one of the places we learn what to feel, when to feel it and towards whom is the playground, so it should come as no surprise that even as adults emotions can be vulnerable to the logic of this space. It takes maturity and some measure of practical wisdom to regulate them not to be so.) We start with an attempt to shame that presupposes shared values, or at the least the possibility of shared values; a few moves later we have pushed one another outside the realm of answerability and descended into mutual contempt.

The narrative logic of emotions is not doomed to be toxic. We can start with a different response and set in train a positive feedback loop. Aly and Stephens point to the example of James Baldwin, whom they believe has been erroneously cited on the side of contempt, but whose work is better read as a refusal of contempt, even towards those who hold you in contempt. On whom falls the burden of breaking cycles of contempt? It is easy to place that burden on those in socially subordinated positions, asking of them a near super-human moral forbearance of not returning contempt with contempt. Alternatively, we might say the burden falls on us all, as the problem comes from all sides. Or we could instead decide that the burden falls asymmetrically – this is not to say that "upward" contempt is better or more readily justified than "downward" contempt, but that it is time for the burden of forbearance to change hands.

Karen Jones

Bo Seo

Aly and Stephens pitch their essay on the ethereal ground of sentiment. "Something's amiss," they write, "isn't it?" The spidey senses are tingling and they intuit a malady in our body politic. Everything – from opinion polls to stray tweets – confirms that initial feeling. Theirs is a sentiment in search of analysis and not an analysis in search of sentiment. And who can blame them? I sense it too. Don't you?

I come to any discussion of polarisation with unclean hands. As a reporter at the *Australian Financial Review*, I wrote many articles on the divisions in our country – including the growth in people's self-reported "dislike" of their political opponents. I authored a book, *Good Arguments*, that trades off a premise shared by Aly and Stephens: our public conversation is in disrepair and we are losing the ability to disagree well.

However, the experience of touring my book around the world and observing Australia from an expatriate's distance has changed my view of polarisation in our country. Based on these reflections, I pose two questions to Aly and Stephens.

First, what are the distinctive features of contemptuous politics in Australia? Aly and Stephens import many examples for their argument from the United States. In so doing, they "do not wish to conflate Australia and the US, but to prevent them becoming more alike." This is a plausible but misleading move. It results in analysis that elides each country's particularities to insinuate proximity – an insinuation which, if anything, may be self-fulfilling.

Living in the United States, I often pause over the particular vulnerabilities of its political system to hyper-partisanship – among them, the contested access to the franchise, the outsized role of campaign finance, and a legal culture fashioned around individual rights and entitlements. I miss, too, the sources of Australia's resistance to such pressures – among them a robust social welfare system and a natural (if begrudging) cosmopolitanism.

What obscures these distinctions in Aly and Stephens' essay is sentiment – the *sense* that things are amiss and that they are amiss in the same way. The authors may be right that the pathologies of social media are universally pervasive. But their unwillingness to explore how these norms interact with particular conditions on the ground results in both a missed opportunity and a fresh danger.

The missed opportunity is the failure to ask what may be distinctive about an Australian expression of contempt. How, for example, might a cultural preference for social equality and distaste for "tall poppies" reinforce or undercut the propensity to dismiss other citizens? The danger is that, in taking our cues from the country "furthest down the road of contempt," we will argue as though we were *there* rather than *here*, and thus enact the resemblance. Building Australia's resistance to contempt requires paying greater attention to the distinctiveness of our political culture – strengths and weaknesses, both.

Second, what is to be done about the problem of contempt? The part of this essay that I wish were longer is Aly and Stephens' prescription of "attentiveness." Instinct in this beautiful instruction are at least three sources of obligation. Sure, we should attend to the "moral reality of other people" for *their* benefit. But we also owe it to ourselves to avoid becoming monstrous in our disregard, and to the "we" that emerges from our relations – whether family, community or nation.

Harder than perceiving the obligation is enacting its demands. In *Good Arguments*, I argue that the art of debating can teach us to disagree better in our everyday lives. Its prescriptions for a more deliberate approach to disputes – naming the disagreement, constructing robust arguments, choosing one's battles – can help us raise our voice and be heard. They evince an attentiveness that stems from the recognition of disagreement as a craft.

Aly and Stephens write that such practices are "inseparable from the democratic aspiration." But it is helpful to separate them to make this point: though we often think aspiration must precede action, the reverse can hold, too. Mutual respect may be less a precondition for a good argument than its outcome – one achieved through noble practice. This inversion puts a finer point on Aly and Stephens' diagnosis: we are not unpractised in the art of disagreeing because we are contemptuous; we are contemptuous because we are so unpractised.

The actions required to counteract contempt need not be solemn. While writing this response, I stumbled on YouTube onto an episode of the joke quiz show *Have You Been Paying Attention?* In the clip, a twenty-something, mullet-haired comedian named Aaron Chen, dressed in a powder-blue tuxedo, was quizzing the prime minister of Australia, Anthony Albanese. "You defeated Scott Morrison. Congratulations. He used to like to be called 'ScoMo,'" Chen drawled. "Will you be called AnAl?"

The line, profane and visceral, was no deep dismissal. It was an invitation from a jester to a ruler to set aside the trappings of high office and engage him as an equal. In my apartment in Cambridge, Massachusetts, I felt as though the summer heat had yielded to a breeze from some distant place. For the moment, the joke cleared the air.

Bo Seo

Waleed Aly & Scott Stephens

Never read the online comments. So goes the advice issued to almost every writer published on a news website. Generally speaking, it's wise. You'll just be infuriated by the ad hominem, the misrepresentations, the people who simply read the headline and post comments that show they never bothered to read any further. But when a portion of our Quarterly Essay was extracted on *The Sydney Morning Herald*'s website, one such comment, usefully – if predictably – presaged what was to come:

> Seems to me, when speaking about the Australian examples, you've chosen your subjects of interest being Julia Gillard, refugees and "Stop Adani" in the context of climate change. Wouldn't a more rounded argument also [have] included the constant bashing of other politicians such as John Howard, the complexities of refugees and why the "Stop Adani" might have been irritating without having to blame the Nationals.

Implicit here is an allegation that we've selectively highlighted examples of right-wing contempt, and that the one exception to this – that of the Stop Adani convoy – was tagged with a dig at the Nationals anyway. That whatever else we were doing, we were revealing our left-wing sympathies. That sort of response, which rummages through the essay, tallies, grades and categorises the examples, and then assigns the overall argument a political persuasion, became relatively commonplace upon its release. So, by the time the correspondence of John Quiggin and Carla Wilshire lodged with us – albeit making a countervailing charge of "right-wing advocacy," in Quiggin's phrase – we were on familiar ground.

And here we were thinking we'd written an essay! Turns out that instead we might have issued a Rorschach test. We'll return to Quiggin and Wilshire, but what's so striking about the highly varied correspondence published here is that it nonetheless falls into a few broad categories that accurately reflect the orientations of the respondents. One group, the philosophers and democratic theorists, take the essay on its terms, consider the implications of contempt for democracy, and then challenge or extend certain of the essay's concepts. Another group, coming from those with more of a culture-war posture, conscript this essay into precisely those wars — rendering it an artefact whose primary value is in whether or not it sides with the right side of those wars. Similarly, but slightly distinctly, stands Nyadol Nyuon's contribution: that of an activist for whom the primary meaning of the essay is what it means for the liberation of the oppressed.

Somewhat apart, though, is Brigid Delaney's vignette, which for all its brevity makes a keen observation. She distils the civic importance of "real" communities in which people are more than their opinions, appear to us more fully in their humanity, and where interdependence demands a kind of supra-political cohesion. These are exactly the things that online conversation doesn't habitually offer. But Delaney's story of a shunned Arkansas pastor offers a prescient warning. It might be that the habits of online engagement have now poisoned our real-world communities, too. Delaney describes this beautifully as a sign of a society "rife with inflammation and division."

That describes a society with a certain condition. And that is fundamentally what our essay is about. A condition. A widely present state of being, an atmosphere — or, in the metaphor the essay adopts, the air. That air, we argue, is thick with a contempt that suffocates democratic culture. And most of our interlocutors — especially those interested in democratic theory — agree. Where they take issue is in how we might best respond, or precisely what the limits might be.

These aren't easy questions. Karen Jones says something uncontroversial by our reckoning when she says white supremacy is "asked and answered." But we can't follow her to her conclusion that we can use "asked and answered" as a test to determine when contempt can safely follow, for precisely the reasons she ends up indicating: the matter of what is "asked and answered" is becoming increasingly the site of politics itself. She gives the conflicts over transgender politics as an example — and it is a good one — but we can observe that political contests are increasingly being framed in that way: contentious issues are presented as resolved, such that all that remains is for others to "educate themselves" or "take the red pill." "Asked and answered" is not a sober description of something, but a move made to foreclose often fledgling debates.

Bo Seo offers us a sharp, quietly thrilling response, suggesting that perhaps we have the problem backwards, and that maybe democratic debate would improve if we gave people the skills to argue better. We're certainly all for imparting those skills, but we have our doubts precisely because of the conditions in which that would be taking place. If we're right that contempt increasingly characterises our common life, then we are dealing with more than a problem of the mind. We're dealing with a problem of the heart. We're up against the fact that our modes of communication incite us to contempt, and that we enjoy hedonic sensations when we indulge in it. Can you get a similar dopamine rush from learning to argue well? Seo might be the expert there, and we'd love to hear from him that you can. But if not, we suspect the starting point would be appreciating that we have a contempt problem in the first place, and considering whether we might actually *want* to argue better.

Or, as Robert Talisse reminds us, we might want to find places where we do things other than argue. Talisse surgically identifies certain conundrums of democracy – among them that it encourages us to build coalitions with other true believers, whose fidelity is best proven by not being fair to their political opponents. On this basis he suggests that our call for attentiveness might commit the mistake of the Addams–Dewey principle: that the solution to any democratic dysfunction is more democracy. But if more democracy means more political engagement and therefore more coalition-building, more democratic activity might in fact increase our mutual contempt, making democratic life worse. And we're inclined to agree. We'd only clarify that ours is not an Addams–Dewey argument. It is one that says democracy is predicated on a kind of civic bond, a mutual recognition of each other as democratic equals and as partners in a shared project with a common future. But we do not say those means are best achieved by making everything at all times a matter of democratic deliberation and contestation. Talisse is right to identify a gap in our essay: there could be a whole other section on the importance of apolitical space as a precondition for healthy political life. There is certainly an argument worth exploring that it is in apolitical life that we become sufficiently real to one another such that we may then be attentive. Delaney, too, gestures in that direction. And if that's correct, it follows that where everything becomes politics, politics must fail.

But the fact that we are discussing a condition means that our essay is not about – and cannot be about – a rogues' gallery of bad actors, because to focus simply on a group of malefactors would be to describe something less than a condition. Clearly this irritates Quiggin, Wilshire, and to a certain extent Nyuon, who want the focus to be very much on certain bad agents – especially the Republican Party in the United States. Hereabouts, the 6 January insurrection is frequently raised, and we stand criticised for not mentioning it in our essay.

We do, actually, on page 55, albeit in passing. True, it doesn't play a major role in our analysis, but that's because ours is not an essay about the specific and particular problems of American politics. It draws heavily on American examples for reasons explained at the outset, but only to the extent that we suspect Australians will see analogues in their own experience. Australia simply has no analogue of 6 January. But we do have analogues of a high-stakes discourse on *Roe v Wade* or any number of culture wars about "bigotry" and "wokery" that we have imported from American social media feeds. Some lengthy consideration of 6 January would have been a mighty digression in a way these other examples are not.

This family of responses therefore put us in something of a bind. Taken together, they charge that the essay's main thrust is to urge the reader that both sides of politics are as bad as each other, and that cancel culture – as the major example of contempt – is a chief threat to democracy, as bad or worse than the 6 January insurrection. Put simply, our bind is this: how far do we go in responding to these charges when they simply don't engage with our essay on its own terms? They are either misrepresentations, misunderstandings or principled refusals to take our argument on face value, preferring instead to uncover its "real" meaning or agenda.

It is true that we draw on examples across the political spectrum. How could it be otherwise in describing a condition? But the question of which side is worse is an irrelevant and uninteresting one when you're diagnosing an emerging, corrosive, increasingly standard mode of discourse. To demand that an essay like this one make such a declaration – and to accuse it of smuggling in right-wing apologia under the cover of faux centrism if it doesn't – is to force it into a pre-existing political disposition in which the apportionment of blame along some political axis must always be the ultimate destination.

Quiggin, Wilshire and Nyuon provide more to engage us when they seem to deny that contempt is a problem *tout court*. For Wilshire, contempt is simply an "individual emotion"; what we should be focusing on is polarisation, and polarisation is the result of inequality. That last point requires further demonstration at a time when Sweden, one of the most equal and high-taxing societies in the world, has a far-right government in its governing coalition, as Denmark previously did for a decade. But the point for our purposes is that this line of argument reflects both a misunderstanding of contempt and of the way the weakening of the bonds of mutuality in the decades following World War II created the political conditions in which many people in the United States, Britain and Australia could fail to be affected by immiseration of their fellow citizens. As Rousseau anticipated, and political philosophers such as John Rawls and Pierre Rosanvallon have argued at great length, contempt precipitates and *enables* pervasive inequality.

(To read the full argument, see Scott Stephens, "Two Towers: How We Learned to Live with Inequality," *Meanjin*, Spring 2017.)

Hereabouts, Nyuon's extraordinary intervention deserves its own, separate and sustained consideration. It is hard not to be impressed by its force and seriousness, and at critical points it can only command our assent. But it is also hard to know how to respond to the imputation of views we do not hold and arguments we did not make. Much like Wilshire, Nyuon says that our essay leaves the impression "that cancel culture and political correctness pose a symmetrical threat, or an even greater threat, to American democracy than Republican attacks on voting rights." Nowhere do we suggest or imply any such thing. To deny a group of people a vote, and therefore a voice, in the constitution of the life of a nation is an egregious act which both humiliates that group by denying them equal status as citizens and undermines any claim to democratic legitimacy. And given the importance we assign throughout the essay to voice and consent, to mutual recognition and the transformative power of civic associations, it is incredible to hold that we would be unconcerned with partisan redistricting, racial disenfranchisement and the ongoing legal assaults on sections 2 and 5 of the *Voting Rights Act* (1965), not to mention the return of voter intimidation and outright political violence. These are vitally important issues, and we are heartened that so many American lawyers and activists, philosophers and politicians are waging a valiant struggle against such blatantly anti-democratic tactics.

But were we to devote significant space in the essay to "Republican attacks on voting rights," Australian readers would have good reason to wonder about its relevance to them. These are the peculiar afflictions of a nation teetering on the brink of becoming a post-democracy, and the product of its particular history of racism and injustice, to say nothing of its fraught relationship to the very idea of political equality and its distinctive (and debased) conception of individual freedom. While Australia certainly has its own share of electoral problems, voter suppression, gerrymandering and an overblown sense of states' rights are not among them. Moreover, we assiduously avoided the attribution of blame to one side of the political divide or the other – Republican or Democrat – not because we hold them equally culpable, nor because we wish to draw some moral equivalence between their conduct, much less take part in a nauseating game of "whataboutism." Politicians and political parties are, at best, a sideshow in our essay; they are epiphenomenal, not really causal. Instead, from the very first sentence we sought to address our fellow citizens, participants all in a shared political project – each one entrusted with the care and cultivation of our common life – and invite them to reflect on the degree to which we have contributed to a prevailing condition of mutual distrust and disdain ("above our wills," as Emerson once put it). Nyuon no doubt would prefer that we focused more of our attention on voter disenfranchisement or white backlash. Fine, but that's a different essay. And, in fairness, we didn't devote much space to "cancel culture" either, and none at all to "political correctness." "Cancel culture" in the essay functions as little more than a ready-to-hand, well-known illustration of the logic of one of the more conspicuous forms of contempt that we adduce – moral contempt – and it would have been strange indeed if we failed to mention it in an essay that sets out to examine the fraying of public deliberation and debate. But we did not linger with it for long. Not for nothing, the instance of "cancel culture" to which we devote the closest attention is the right-wing media's censure of Yassmin Abdel-Magied. That seems to have gone unremarked.

More troubling, by far, is Nyuon's claim that the form of moral reasoning we employ in the essay against the prevalence of contempt "echoes the historical justifications used to restrain and even reverse progress, especially as demanded by the historically marginalised (the contemned)." In effect, she charges us with peddling what Martin Luther King Jr called "the tranquilizing drug of gradualism" – his way of characterising the pseudo-prudential efforts on the part of effete northern moderates in the 1960s to impede the progress of voting rights legislation for fear that such legislation would prove too disruptive to an untenable status quo. But King insisted that this kind of political stability is unjust, because its cost was too high and had to be borne by too few: it entailed nothing less than consigning black women and men to a state of moral suffocation, condemning them to inexpressiveness by denying them access to the democratic medium in which their voices could be heard and their consent given.

But for King, there were two insidious threats to the cause of racial equality. One was the bromide of "gradualism," which promised that the desired change would come, eventually, and even then only at a rate white Americans could stand. The other was what King called a "new militancy," which viewed white Americans as "the enemy," as an existential threat to their wellbeing, and therefore portrayed their struggle for justice as a zero-sum contest. King believed that both temptations had to be avoided at every turn if the nation was to be made whole – if American democracy was to become a moral reality. And so, from the passage of the *Voting Rights Act* in 1965 until his assassination in 1968, King would condemn with commensurate urgency the reversion to violence and contempt on the part of black militants as the self-defeating pursuit of purportedly just ends through patently unjust means, *and* the self-serving callousness of the "great majority of Americans" who are "uneasy with injustice but unwilling yet to pay a significant price to eradicate it." Both, he urged, must be renounced in order to cultivate the proper moral emotions between citizens such that they could come to see themselves as constituting one people who share one another's future and bear one another's fate – a "beloved community." As Tommie Shelby puts it, King insisted that we "should not be content with interracial *detente*; we should strive for interracial civic friendship."

However much Martin Luther King is revered now, his message of "interracial civic friendship" and his call for the renunciation of racial contempt proved to be fabulously unpopular, as Nyuon observes. In a 1968 Gallup poll, King ranked fifth on the list of "least trusted" public figures; he was "disapproved of" by more than 75 per cent of white Americans, and more than 60 per cent of black Americans. By contrast, according to the same poll, the brazenly segregationist governor of Alabama, George Wallace, who was running for president as a third-party candidate, came in eighth on the list of the "most trusted" Americans. Contempt, clearly, can be popular. But the point isn't popularity. There are doubtless many effective means of achieving restitution for the crimes of the past, ways of seizing power and forcing the hand of "History." What King insisted is that democracy imposes certain inherent constraints on what means might be employed if the goal truly is justice *as equality* and mutual recognition – because (as we cite in the essay) "the end is pre-existent in the means, and ultimately destructive means cannot bring about constructive ends."

You can argue for a different politics if you like, in which just ends license unrestricted means. But at that point, you are not arguing for a democratic politics. And you immediately raise questions that never really receive an answer. For instance: precisely which means of activism are you prepared to endorse? At what point would you deem certain means illegitimate even in the face of injustice, and on what basis would you proscribe them, especially if "what is being protested" is "the problem" rather than "the manner of protest"? And precisely what conditions describe the end point at which we can say means matter as much as ends? Our democracy is a long way from a world of legalised slavery, segregation and the denial of the vote. Can a politics of means resume then? Or must some absolute equality exist first?

We may not have written the essay that Nyuon wanted, but does that really warrant lumping us in with the opponents of racial justice? Is there really any suggestion in our essay that we are trying to pump the brakes of progress lest "the contemned" demand too much too quickly and hurt too many feelings along the way? Is it really our position that those who are demanding radical change need to "play nice" so as to ensure they can be safely ignored? Or is it simply that fidelity to a democratic vision of the preciousness of persons and the demands of justice places certain moral requirements on speech and conduct to which citizens must aspire if they want to sustain a life in common? By characterising our position as she did, Nyuon unfortunately engages in precisely the form of argument about which we warn throughout the essay, whereby those with whom one disagrees are caricatured, tossed into the same basket as some truly bad actors, pronounced guilty by association, and dismissed altogether.

This applies equally to her crass dismissal of Immanuel Kant, reducing the contribution of his moral philosophy to some notorious remarks in the notes to his 1781–82 lectures on anthropology in which he proposed a kind of hierarchy of races and offered a principled defence of colonialism. While these views were omitted from the subsequent publication of his lectures, they were reiterated, to varying degrees, in lectures and papers and in a number of letters written during the 1780s and early 1790s. There is no defending or excusing them. But what Nyuon fails to mention is that Kant would himself go on to repudiate these very views in the late 1790s: he condemned the colonial seizure of lands and labour, upheld the importance of contracts and informed consent with the indigenous occupants of non-European territories, argued that the interests and wellbeing of indigenous populations imposed a normative constraint on the designs and conduct of Europeans, and denounced the utter inhumanity of chattel slavery in *Toward Perpetual Peace* (1795) and in *The Metaphysics of Morals* (1797) – which, incidentally, also contains his most fully developed reflections on the non-reduction of human beings to means to another's end, and on the vice of holding other human beings in contempt. And it is precisely this refusal of contempt that, in a very real way, made his repudiation of colonialism possible.

We did not use Kant in the essay as a source of authority, much less a trump card, but as someone who bears persuasive witness to a vision of human community founded on the preciousness and equality of persons, in which each is called to consider the interests of others and to adopt the kind of dispositions and quotidian habits that would permit their life together to grow in depth and mutual understanding. It is a vision that can lay claim to no authority apart from the terms of its own appeal – which is to say, the invitation it holds out to see the world, and those within it, in a different, more gracious light. Like philosophy, democracy has no claim to authority apart of the consent of citizens and is assured by nothing other than their daily willingness to go on together. This is, of course, an invitation that may be rejected: there are those who will refuse the moral constraints inherent to a democratic vision of life, and eschew the very notion of pursuing a future in which their enemies have a place. No wonder, as Stanley

Cavell puts it, philosophy and democracy seem both to vacillate perpetually between hope and despair.

Is there any better way of characterising the moral vision of James Baldwin than as one which occupies the space between hope and despair? Nyuon rightly observes the importance of Baldwin's witness in our essay, but her contention seems to be that we illegitimately appropriate him, turning him into a shill for our own purposes – our very own Booker T. Washington (or Herschel Walker) in the service of a kind of counter-revolution to the cause of racial justice. There's no point engaging in a contest of duelling Baldwin quotes, for his writing, like his life, "refuses summation," as Toni Morrison put it in her eulogy at his funeral. Even in his own time, Baldwin was a highly controversial figure, more even than King, because he fit neatly nowhere. He could be claimed by no one, and easily enlisted in no cause. He was black and bisexual, but refused the mythologies of black nationalism and the cultural reification of what he termed "queer identity"; a Baptist preacher's son, and a child evangelist himself, who abandoned Christianity; a son of Harlem who lived much of his life in France and Istanbul; a close friend and ally of Martin Luther King and Malcolm X, and yet a loving critic of both; neither a secular saint nor an activist, but a writer who made his name with an incendiary critique of the most revered black novelist of the first half of the twentieth century; a public intellectual whose public standing collapsed in 1968, in part because of Eldridge Cleaver's mercilessly homophobic attacks. Cleaver charged Baldwin, among other things, with relinquishing his black manhood on account of his sexuality, and wrote that Baldwin was trying to become "a white man in a black body." For Cleaver, a Black Panther leader, Baldwin's refusal of contempt was simply appeasement, an attempt to ingratiate himself with whites. And when the violence which engulfed 110 American cities after King's assassination was taken to demand either total justification or absolute condemnation, Baldwin refused to do either. But this is precisely why Baldwin demands attention in a time like ours: the way his life and writing straddled what would seem to be incommensurable positions bears vital witness to his determination to escape America's suffocating cycle of racial contempt and counter-contempt.

That cycle invites us to recall an aspect of Baldwin's thought to which our interlocutors paid insufficient attention. That to succumb to contempt is to license it per se, and thereby to consent to the other's contempt for one's self. Nyuon asks if "the moral responsibility for resisting contempt ... is only imposed on the contemned"? We'd suggest our answer was unequivocal: no, it is imposed on all. That is precisely the moral basis on which the contemned can protest their contemning. But as Baldwin understood, something fundamental changes when contempt becomes the coin of the realm. It then circulates in all directions, including – perhaps especially – among those seeking equality. So, members of the Nation of Islam ended up being the ones who assassinated Malcolm X. Baldwin's own treatment at the hands of Cleaver is another illustration. Or, to choose a contemporary, local example, allegations of an Indigenous senator leaving an Indigenous elder traumatised by a tirade of abuse after a meeting at Parliament House. Even the dynamics of cancel culture illustrate this. Progressives can't cancel Donald Trump or his supporters. They thrive on that. The ones who truly fear being cancelled are most often fellow travellers. Twitter pile-ons frequently take that form: feminists castigating other feminists for being the wrong kind of feminist; progressive stoushes on transgender issues; Muslim activists tearing apart senior, even revered, Muslim scholars. And of course, as we quoted Jonathan Haidt noting, Republicans attacking their colleagues as "cuckservatives."

If our reading of Baldwin is "overstretched," as she claims, then Nyuon's reading is indefensibly narrow. Take the example of Baldwin's use of the term "innocence." Anyone who has read Baldwin knows that "white innocence" in his writing does not suggest guiltlessness, much less a kind of spurious moral purity. Rather, it denotes something closer to self-delusion, a wilful ignorance as to white Americans' complicity in the immiseration of their fellow human beings. The moral force of Baldwin's use of the term "innocence" is thus analogous to Ralph Waldo Emerson's description of the self-satisfied lives of the inhabitants of the "civilized" northern states prior to the Civil War: they may be far removed from the barbarity of the plantation, and yet the delicacies on which they dine each evening and the comforts with which they adorn themselves each day are the products of a regime of systemic degradation. It is their "graceful distance" from that suffering which permits them to live in a kind of effete oblivion to the "dreadful debt" they owe to the slaves who picked the cotton and boiled the sugarcane. As Emerson puts it, unforgettably, "The sugar they raised was excellent: nobody tasted blood in it." Like Emerson's neighbours, Baldwin's fellow citizens liked to believe themselves untouched by the taint of injustice. And yet this will-not-to-know had consigned them, Baldwin thought, to a state of perpetual adolescence; it had retarded their moral growth and bound them to an infantilising self-image from which they must be freed.

As Baldwin writes in No Name in the Street, "the fraudulent and expedient nature of the American innocence ... has always been able to persuade itself that it does not know what it knows too well." But even here, the term "innocence" is inflected with a mixture of bewilderment and pity, not condescension, certainly not contempt. The contempt with which white Americans have viewed their black brothers and sisters has so distorted their vision that they cannot even see themselves clearly. That, for Baldwin, is what contempt does: it leads to the moral deformation of the eyes. Which is why, after he writes, "Whoever debases others is debasing himself," he explains immediately: "That is not a mystical statement but a most realistic one, which is proved by the eyes of any Alabama sheriff – and I would not like to see Negroes ever arrive at so wretched a condition." The only thing that can free the "white man" from the self-imposed anguish of his "innocence," the only thing that can release him "from the tyranny of his mirror," Baldwin writes, is to "be seen as he is ... by those who are not white." He goes on:

> All of us know, whether or not we are able to admit it, that mirrors can only lie, that death by drowning is all that awaits one there. It is for this reason that love is so desperately sought and so cunningly avoided. Love takes off the masks we fear we cannot live without and know we cannot live within. I use the word "love" here not merely in the personal sense but as a state of being, or a state of grace – not in the infantile American sense of being made happy but in the tough and universal sense of quest and daring and growth.

For Baldwin, love is the contrary of contempt. It creates the conditions in which the parties can realise a life, and a just future, together. Whereas the contempt he heard in the words of Elijah Muhammad – as Baldwin dined with him at the headquarters of the Nation of Islam movement on Chicago's South Side – represented to him "the absolute death of the communication which might help to liberate both Negroes and whites." Nyuon is right that there is nothing "romantic" or sentimental about Baldwin's notion of love, but it is nonetheless passionate, and not simply political.

Which delivers us, finally, to Martin Krygier's strong suggestion that we would have been better off, and our readers better served, had we simply adopted the language of civility rather than that of "love" or "attentiveness." In a sense, he is unarguably correct. Civility is the *horizontal* expression of our shared commitment to political equality – it is how we show that we regard one another as equals. As such, civility is the name for the particular type of moral restraint that must be reciprocally exercised by members of a democratic community if their deliberations and disagreements over the state of their common life are to remain non-coercive. To put it bluntly: without civility, there is no consent. And so, for Stanley Cavell, civility "is not a particular moral demand, but the condition of democratic morality." This is not to reduce civility to courtesy, much less politeness. Rather, it suggests a way of speaking which ensures that our speech is answerable to others. In his important book *Sustaining Democracy*, Robert Talisse puts it this way:

> Civility is consistent with hostility and rancor; one need not like others in order to duly recognize their equality. Congeniality and fondness are not necessary for civility. All that civility requires is that citizens do not lose sight of the fact that their fellow citizens are their political equals, who are therefore entitled to an equal say.

Our thinking on civility and democratic equality has been richly informed by Talisse, Teresa Bejan and Danielle Allen, among others, and we've discussed their work (occasionally with them) on numerous episodes of *The Minefield*. But in the essay, we steered clear of the language of "civility" for reasons made clear by Carla Wilshire's correspondence: because civility has already become so widely associated with politeness, and so widely – though we say wrongly – attacked as a structure of oppression in itself. We hoped that by transposing the language of our essay into a different and perhaps unexpected key – contempt, attentiveness, love, reciprocal devotion, marriage – it might give our sense of the problem and of the solution (much of which resonates with the sentiments expressed by Philip Selznick) a wider hearing.

Perhaps Krygier is right, and this will prove to have been a failed and ulti-mately fanciful endeavour. Maybe contempt is simply too much the air we breathe, and democracies such as the United States, Britain and Australia have already passed the point of no return. But if there remains some hope, we believe it begins with a recommitment to the task of *attentiveness*, which is why we are prepared to linger with the analogy between democracy and marriage. "Recip-rocal devotion" perhaps misleadingly conjures the image of citizens looking lovingly in one another's eyes, as if such strong emotions could be cultivated, much less realised, in a diverse political community "whom chance or choice have brought together" (to quote Michael Oakeshott). This is not what we argued. Rather, the devotedness is to the condition of political communality itself, as an expression of the desire that it should persist – and that it should persist with our opponents as an indispensable part. Writing in the early nineteenth century, the philosopher Georg Hegel was convinced that marriages pass from "contingency" (two random people bound together by nothing more than a kind of contract) to "necessity" (an enduring ethical bond) only when each person comes to see themselves through the other's eyes as a person worthy of love. Is it really too much to suggest that the commitment to see one another as equals, and therefore as equal participants in a shared political project which depends on cooperation, compromise, frankness, remorse, forgiveness, reciprocity and mutual education, requires a devotion for which the only word is love?

Waleed Aly & Scott Stephens

Waleed Aly is a writer, academic, lawyer and broadcaster. He is a lecturer in politics at Monash University and co-host of Network Ten's *The Project*. He is the author of *People Like Us* and Quarterly Essay 37, *What's Right?*.

Brigid Delaney is the author of *Wellmania*, *This Restless Life*, *Wild Things* and a book explaining Stoic philosophy – *Reasons Not to Worry*. She has worked as a columnist and journalist for *Guardian Australia* and is currently a speechwriter for a federal minister.

Karen Jones is an associate professor of philosophy at the University of Melbourne. She has written extensively on trust, what it is and when it is justified. She also writes on emotion and rationality. Much of her work is from a feminist perspective.

Martin Krygier is a professor of law and social theory at UNSW, and a senior research fellow at the CEU Democracy Institute, Budapest. Among his writings is *Civil Passions*, published by Black Inc. in 2005. His most recent publication is *Anti-Constitutional Populism*, co-edited with Adam Czarnota and Wojciech Sadurski.

Katharine Murphy has worked in Canberra's parliamentary press gallery since 1996, for the *Australian Financial Review*, *The Australian* and *The Age*, before joining *Guardian Australia*, where she is political editor. She is the author of *On Disruption* and a previous Quarterly Essay, *The End of Certainty*.

Nyadol Nyuon is a commercial litigator and community advocate. She was born in Ethiopia and raised in Kenya, and moved to Australia at age eighteen. In 2011 and 2014, Nyadol was nominated as one of the 100 most influential African-Australians. She is a board member of the Melbourne Social Equity Institute and appears regularly in the media, including on ABC's *The Drum* and *Q&A*.

John Quiggin is a professor of economics at the University of Queensland. He is a regular commentator in traditional and social media. His most recent book is *Economics in Two Lessons: Why Markets Work So Well and Why They Can Fail So Badly*.

Bo Seo is a student at Harvard Law School and a former journalist at the *Australian Financial Review*. His book, *Good Arguments*, is slated for publication in nine languages.

Scott Stephens is the ABC's Religion and Ethics online editor. He is widely published on moral philosophy and has edited volumes of the writings of Slovenian philosopher Slavoj Žižek and Australian philosopher Raimond Gaita. With Waleed Aly, he co-hosts *The Minefield* on ABC Radio National.

Robert B. Talisse is an American philosopher and political theorist. He is a professor of philosophy at Vanderbilt University and the author of several books, including *Sustaining Democracy: What We Owe to the Other Side*.

Carla Wilshire is the founding CEO of the Social Policy Group. She has worked in senior roles in the public service and as an adviser to government, principally in migration and settlement, including as chief of staff to ministers for multicultural affairs, innovation and sport.

WANT THE LATEST FROM QUARTERLY ESSAY?

THE RECKONING
HOW #METOO IS CHANGING AUSTRALIA
JESS HILL

Correspondence
'TOP BLOKES' Rachel Nolan, Bri Lee, David Hunt,
Alison Pennington, Shannon Burns, Elizabeth Flux,
Tom Lee, Vivian Gerrand, Lech Blaine

SLEEPWALK TO WAR
AUSTRALIA'S UNTHINKING ALLIANCE WITH AMERICA
HUGH WHITE

Correspondence
'NOT WAVING, DROWNING' Rick Morton,
Jennifer Doggett, Russell Marks, Janet McCalman,
Nicola Redhouse, James Dunk, John Kuot, Joo-Inn
Chew, Alexandra Goldsworthy, Sebastian Rosenberg,
Sarah Krasnostein

**Subscribe to the Friends of Quarterly Essay
email newsletter to share in news, updates,
events and special offers.**

quarterlyessay.com.au/signup

QUARTERLY ESSAY
BACK ISSUES

BACK ISSUES: (Prices include GST, postage and handling within Australia.) *Grey indicates out of stock.*

- [ ] **QE 1** ($17.99) Robert Manne *In Denial*
- [ ] **QE 2** ($17.99) John Birmingham *Appeasing Jakarta*
- [ ] **QE 3** ($17.99) Guy Rundle *The Opportunist*
- [ ] **QE 4** ($17.99) Don Watson *Rabbit Syndrome*
- [ ] **QE 5** ($17.99) Mungo MacCallum *Girt By Sea*
- [ ] **QE 6** ($17.99) John Button *Beyond Belief*
- [ ] **QE 7** ($17.99) John Martinkus *Paradise Betrayed*
- [ ] **QE 8** ($17.99) Amanda Lohrey *Groundswell*
- [ ] **QE 9** ($17.99) Tim Flannery *Beautiful Lies*
- [ ] **QE 10** ($17.99) Gideon Haigh *Bad Company*
- [ ] **QE 11** ($17.99) Germaine Greer *Whitefella Jump Up*
- [ ] **QE 12** ($17.99) David Malouf *Made in England*
- [ ] **QE 13** ($17.99) Robert Manne with David Corlett *Sending Them Home*
- [ ] **QE 14** ($17.99) Paul McGeough *Mission Impossible*
- [ ] **QE 15** ($17.99) Margaret Simons *Latham's World*
- [ ] **QE 16** ($17.99) Raimond Gaita *Breach of Trust*
- [ ] **QE 17** ($17.99) John Hirst *'Kangaroo Court'*
- [ ] **QE 18** ($17.99) Gail Bell *The Worried Well*
- [ ] **QE 19** ($17.99) Judith Brett *Relaxed & Comfortable*
- [ ] **QE 20** ($17.99) John Birmingham *A Time for War*
- [ ] **QE 21** ($17.99) Clive Hamilton *What's Left?*
- [ ] **QE 22** ($17.99) Amanda Lohrey *Voting for Jesus*
- [ ] **QE 23** ($17.99) Inga Clendinnen *The History Question*
- [ ] **QE 24** ($17.99) Robyn Davidson *No Fixed Address*
- [ ] **QE 25** ($17.99) Peter Hartcher *Bipolar Nation*
- [ ] **QE 26** ($17.99) David Marr *His Master's Voice*
- [ ] **QE 27** ($17.99) Ian Lowe *Reaction Time*
- [ ] **QE 28** ($17.99) Judith Brett *Exit Right*
- [ ] **QE 29** ($17.99) Anne Manne *Love & Money*
- [ ] **QE 30** ($17.99) Paul Toohey *Last Drinks*
- [ ] **QE 31** ($17.99) Tim Flannery *Now or Never*
- [ ] **QE 32** ($17.99) Kate Jennings *American Revolution*
- [ ] **QE 33** ($17.99) Guy Pearse *Quarry Vision*
- [ ] **QE 34** ($17.99) Annabel Crabb *Stop at Nothing*
- [ ] **QE 35** ($17.99) Noel Pearson *Radical Hope*
- [ ] **QE 36** ($17.99) Mungo MacCallum *Australian Story*
- [ ] **QE 37** ($17.99) Waleed Aly *What's Right?*
- [ ] **QE 38** ($17.99) David Marr *Power Trip*
- [ ] **QE 39** ($17.99) Hugh White *Power Shift*
- [ ] **QE 40** ($17.99) George Megalogenis *Trivial Pursuit*
- [ ] **QE 41** ($17.99) David Malouf *The Happy Life*
- [ ] **QE 42** ($17.99) Judith Brett *Fair Share*
- [ ] **QE 43** ($17.99) Robert Manne *Bad News*
- [ ] **QE 44** ($17.99) Andrew Charlton *Man-Made World*
- [ ] **QE 45** ($17.99) Anna Krien *Us and Them*
- [ ] **QE 46** ($17.99) Laura Tingle *Great Expectations*
- [ ] **QE 47** ($17.99) David Marr *Political Animal*
- [ ] **QE 48** ($17.99) Tim Flannery *After the Future*
- [ ] **QE 49** ($17.99) Mark Latham *Not Dead Yet*
- [ ] **QE 50** ($17.99) Anna Goldsworthy *Unfinished Business*
- [ ] **QE 51** ($17.99) David Marr *The Prince*
- [ ] **QE 52** ($17.99) Linda Jaivin *Found in Translation*
- [ ] **QE 53** ($17.99) Paul Toohey *That Sinking Feeling*
- [ ] **QE 54** ($17.99) Andrew Charlton *Dragon's Tail*
- [ ] **QE 55** ($17.99) Noel Pearson *A Rightful Place*
- [ ] **QE 56** ($17.99) Guy Rundle *Clivosaurus*
- [ ] **QE 57** ($17.99) Karen Hitchcock *Dear Life*
- [ ] **QE 58** ($17.99) David Kilcullen *Blood Year*
- [ ] **QE 59** ($17.99) David Marr *Faction Man*
- [ ] **QE 60** ($17.99) Laura Tingle *Political Amnesia*
- [ ] **QE 61** ($17.99) George Megalogenis *Balancing Act*
- [ ] **QE 62** ($17.99) James Brown *Firing Line*
- [ ] **QE 63** ($17.99) Don Watson *Enemy Within*
- [ ] **QE 64** ($17.99) Stan Grant *The Australian Dream*
- [ ] **QE 65** ($17.99) David Marr *The White Queen*
- [ ] **QE 66** ($17.99) Anna Krien *The Long Goodbye*
- [ ] **QE 67** ($17.99) Benjamin Law *Moral Panic 101*
- [ ] **QE 68** ($17.99) Hugh White *Without America*
- [ ] **QE 69** ($17.99) Mark McKenna *Moment of Truth*
- [ ] **QE 70** ($17.99) Richard Denniss *Dead Right*
- [ ] **QE 71** ($17.99) Laura Tingle *Follow the Leader*
- [ ] **QE 72** ($17.99) Sebastian Smee *Net Loss*
- [ ] **QE 73** ($17.99) Rebecca Huntley *Australia Fair*
- [ ] **QE 74** ($17.99) Erik Jensen *The Prosperity Gospel*
- [ ] **QE 75** ($17.99) Annabel Crabb *Men at Work*
- [ ] **QE 76** ($17.99) Peter Hartcher *Red Flag*
- [ ] **QE 77** ($17.99) Margaret Simons *Cry Me a River*
- [ ] **QE 78** ($17.99) Judith Brett *The Coal Curse*
- [ ] **QE 79** ($17.99) Katharine Murphy *The End of Certainty*
- [ ] **QE 80** ($17.99) Laura Tingle *The High Road*
- [ ] **QE 81** ($17.99) Alan Finkel *Getting to Zero*
- [ ] **QE 82** ($17.99) George Megalogenis *Exit Strategy*
- [ ] **QE 83** ($17.99) Lech Blaine *Top Blokes*
- [ ] **QE 84** ($17.99) Jess Hill *The Reckoning*
- [ ] **QE 85** ($24.99) Sarah Krasnostein *Not Waving, Drowning*
- [ ] **QE 86** ($24.99) Hugh White *Sleepwalk to War*
- [ ] **QE 87** ($24.99) Waleed Aly & Scott Stephens *Uncivil Wars*

Please include this form with delivery and payment details overleaf.
Back issues also available as eBooks at **quarterlyessay.com**

SUBSCRIBE TO RECEIVE
10% OFF THE COVER PRICE

DELIVERY AND PAYMENT DETAILS